Prayers
that get
RESULTS

Prayers
that get
RESULTS

Tom Brown

WHITAKER
HOUSE

PRAYERS THAT GET RESULTS

Tom Brown
P.O. Box 27275
El Paso, TX 79926
(915) 855-9673 / www.tbm.org

ISBN: 978-1-60374-562-8
Printed in the United States of America
© 2012 by Tom Brown

Whitaker House
1030 Hunt Valley Circle
New Kensington, PA 15068
www.whitakerhouse.com

Library of Congress Cataloging-in-Publication Data (pending)

1 2 3 4 5 6 7 8 9 10 11 ⊔ 19 18 17 16 15 14 13 12

Contents

Introduction

I can't claim that every prayer of mine has been answered, but I have learned enough from the Bible and experience to be able to rejoice greatly for the many answers my prayers *have* received.

I think of Julian, a nine-year-old boy who had been born blind. His mother brought him to the Good Friday service at my church in El Paso, Texas. As I prayed for him, I used a prayer found in Scripture: *"Stretch out your hand to heal and perform miraculous signs and wonders through the name of your holy servant Jesus"* (Acts 4:30). As soon as I said that prayer, God opened Julian's eyes. He could see! His mother brought him to the platform and wept as she testified to her son's healing. I talked with Julian, and I asked him, "Can you really see?" Julian nodded and began to cry with joy, because God had opened his eyes. There was not a dry eye in the entire church. The people there had witnessed a real miracle of biblical proportion.

I also remember Ron. He had recently gotten saved and had been attending our church for several weeks. He came to me after a Sunday service and said, "Pastor Brown, I want so much for my wife, Margaret, to experience what I have with the Lord. But she doesn't seem interested."

I showed him Matthew 18:19, *"If two of you on earth agree about anything you ask for, it will be done for you by my*

Father in heaven," and we began to pray. I felt led by the Lord to pray that Ron's wife would be saved the following Sunday. After our prayer, I asked Ron to tell his wife that Pastor Brown had prayed for her salvation and that she was going to become saved the very next Sunday. He did exactly what I asked him to. The following week, I saw Ron come into church for the Sunday service, accompanied for the first time by his wife. Margaret was saved that day. She later told me that she had been curious about attending church because of my boldness in announcing that she would get saved. Since that day, Ron and Margaret have served faithfully as leaders in our church.

Through my prayers, I have seen incurable sicknesses healed, witnessed the hardest of sinners saved, received wisdom in the most confusing of situations, won favor with my adversaries, been given unexpected money to meet a need, watched the demon possessed return to their normal minds, and observed intimacy restored to loveless marriages.

Nothing is impossible with God when we pray effectively. The key word is *effectively.* Anyone can pray, but far too few Christians know how to pray effectively. The Bible says, *"The prayer of a righteous man* [or woman!] *is powerful and effective"* (James 5:16). The word *"powerful"* means "mighty, without limits." Nothing is too difficult or beyond God's ability to change. And the word *"effective"* means "able to produce the intended results." *Results* are what we are after in this book.

A Primary Purpose of Prayer

Carl had just received news from his doctor that he had a malignant tumor and that he had only six months left to live. Carl needed God to miraculously heal him.

Betsy found out that her husband was seeing another woman and was planning to divorce her. Betsy needed God to change her husband.

John and Mary had discovered that their son was taking drugs. They needed their son to be freed from the bondage of addiction.

Ralph had been laid off and didn't know how he was going to provide for his family. Ralph needed a job.

Cecilia discovered the reason for her mood swings when she was diagnosed with manic depression. Cecilia needed God to break the spirit of depression.

Lauren had been presented with an opportunity that had the potential to either make him a great deal of money or bankrupt him completely. Lauren needed wisdom.

Pastor Jacob was crushed because the city wouldn't give his church the building permit it needed to expand. Pastor Jacob needed God's favor with the city council.

Angelina was devastated to hear that she was not able to bear children. Angelina needed her womb healed.

These people may remind you of situations in your own life. It is troubles like these that drive us to pray. While trouble should not be the only thing that compels us to pray to God, let's not fool ourselves; trouble in life has a way of bringing us to our knees. As the Bible says, *"Is any one of you in trouble? He should pray"* (James 5:13). One of the primary purposes of prayer is to ask God to deliver us from trouble.

How This Book Is Arranged

This book is divided into three parts. Part I explores a variety of prayers in depth, showing how they relate to specific circumstances and cover certain needs. Not all prayers are the same. One prayer may work better for health, while another one may work better for marriage. You need to know what kind of prayer to pray for each situation. Part II examines why some prayers go unanswered and details common mistakes Christians often make when they pray. Part III deals with the steps you can take to receive answers to your prayers. The book concludes with an overview of the Lord's Prayer. In a matter of just a few chapters, you will be on your way to praying effectively. In its entirety, this book is meant to help you develop a deeper prayer life characterized by longer, more meaningful prayers.

Perhaps you have not enjoyed praying; it feels more like a chore. Of course, that's only natural when you are not seeing results. But, once you begin to see your prayers answered, it will be hard for you *not* to pray. You'll be praying as much as physically possible once you understand how to pray in a way that receives answers. Again, this book is all about results.

If you are interested in praying only out of a desire to sound religious, this book is not for you. But, if you are longing to see your prayers answered, you have found the right resource. Let's embark on this exciting journey to the limitless realm of prayer!

Part I

Different Types of Prayer

Chapter 1

The Prayer of Submission

"Abba, Father," he said, "everything is possible for you. Take this
cup from me. Yet not what I will, but what you will."
—Mark 14:36

The end was near. Jesus had finished His teaching and healing mission; now, it was time to complete His sacrificial mission. The cross was before Him. He knew it meant that He
would be separated from the Father. But He also knew that
this was the reason He had come to earth. He had to take
the sin of the world upon Himself. Could there be any other
way? Maybe salvation could be achieved without a sacrifice.
His wish for another way gave Him some hope that, perhaps,
one existed. The only thing for Him to do was to pray. And
pray He did.

Imagine what this scene must have been like. He asked
three of His disciples to pray with Him. He felt the weight of
the world on His shoulders. His spirit was in agony. He could
take it no longer; He fell to His knees. Before He uttered
anything too quickly, He paused for a moment and considered God's love for Him. God was His Father! He knew that.
Then, He began to contemplate the power of God. Anything
was possible with Him—He knew that, also. With these

two great truths, He opened His mouth and asked God for a contingency plan: *"'Abba, Father,' he said, 'everything is possible for you. Take this cup from me'"* (Mark 14:36). There was still some hope that God would make another way. Yet, His mind was pressed by the nagging thought that the cross was God's only way. Then, He prayed a prayer of submission, saying, *"Yet not what I will, but what you will"* (Mark 14:36).

This single prayer did not satisfy Jesus. He prayed the same words again with slight adjustments. Nothing changed, other than His disciples' falling asleep, despite His request that they keep watch with Him. (See, for example, Mark 14:37–41.) The disciples did not sense the urgency of the moment. Christ alone knew what was about to happen. After realizing He had been left alone to pray, Jesus prayed a second time, but, in this case, His words suggested resignation: *"My Father, if it is not possible for this cup to be taken away unless I drink it, may your will be done"* (Matthew 26:42). After this, a third time He prayed, *"saying the same thing"* (Matthew 26:44). With those final words, His prayer was answered—not in the removing of the cup but in His receiving the strength and comfort He needed. An angel appeared and gave Him the power He sought to fulfill the will of God. (See Luke 22:43.)

The prayer of submission is the most important type of prayer because it is the foundation of all other kinds of prayer. Unless you learn to pray the prayer of submission, none of the other types of prayer will work for you.

A Life Submitted to God

Jesus' prayer in the garden of Gethsemane was not the only time when He submitted Himself to the Father. In fact, His entire life was an act of submission. The writer of Hebrews recorded what Jesus said regarding His entry into the world: *"I have come to do your will, O God"* (Hebrews 10:7). Jesus did not come to the earth for Himself; He came to serve the Father. Thus, the purpose of prayer is never to accomplish human will but always to bring God's will to fruition. If you approach prayer as a means to an end—the meeting of your personal desires—you're missing the point. You must see prayer as a process of linking yourself with God so that He can work through you. Any other understanding is inferior and even erroneous.

In fact, the reason God answered every prayer of Christ's—prayers to heal, prayers to raise the dead, prayers to calm storms, prayers to drive out demons, prayers to save the lost—was that Jesus was submitting Himself through prayer. As the writer of Hebrews explained it, *"During the days of Jesus' life on earth, he offered up prayers and petitions with loud cries and tears to the one who could save him from death, and he was heard because of his reverent submission"* (Hebrews 5:7). You can ask God for anything, and He will give it to you, but only if your life is submitted to Him.

Learning to Submit

The main purpose of the prayer of submission is to overcome personal temptations and sins. So often, believers pray for more money or for healing, forgetting that the most important thing to pray for is help in overcoming sin. The prayer of submission was designed for this request.

In this fallen world, all of us are continually tempted to go our own way, to do our own thing. The disciples did just this after Jesus was arrested. Peter struck the ear of the servant of

16 *Prayers That Get Results*

the high priest, who was among those who had come to take Him, while the others scattered in fear. They responded in the flesh because they had failed to pray along with Christ that they would not fall into temptation. Prayer could have kept them in the Spirit. We fall into temptation not because we are weak or the temptation is too strong but because we have not prayed as we should have. Effective prayers, especially prayers of submission, keep us walking in the will of God.

Listen to the Lord, Not Man

I was teaching at a Full Gospel Business Men's Fellowship meeting where I shared my story of salvation and being called into ministry. As I did, I noticed one man who seemed to be especially affected by my message. He was tall, with thinning blond hair, and he was hanging on my every word. After the meeting, he came up to me and introduced himself. "Hello, I'm Barney Field," he said. "Your story touched me. I am a businessman, and I'm totally dissatisfied with what I'm doing. I feel a call into ministry, but, to obey God, I would have to sell my business and lose a steady income. I don't know what to do."

Many people would have advised Barney to stay in business, because, after all, there is a need for Christian businesspeople, just as there is a need for more Christian pastors. Other people might have cautioned Barney, asking him if he was not mistaken that he had heard God's call into ministry. But I know that God often calls us to do difficult things, just as Jesus called all of His disciples to leave everything and follow Him. (See, for example, Matthew 8:19–22.) I said to Barney, "You have to pray and tell God that you are willing to obey Him, no matter the cost. God will give you the strength and provision you need to obey." Then, we prayed together.

I am so glad I gave the response that I did. He was obedient, and today, Barney Field is a leading minister in our city, a man who encourages fellow pastors and other churches to emulate godliness. Together, he and I have been instrumental in opposing the radical gay agenda our city's politicians have been promoting. Barney Field is a great example of the power of the prayer of submission.

Society does not encourage submission. Instead, our culture says, "Be your own person!" and "Do your own thing!" The prevailing mind-set does not make God a priority or view Him with reverence.

Prioritize God's Agenda above Your Personal Desires

To really pray the prayer of submission, you must see most of your desires as they truly are—opposed to God's. You have to admit that your flesh is weak. Too often, we think we are strong in our own power, and we assume that we are naturally prone to do the right thing. The Bible begs to differ. It tells us that mankind is in opposition to God. Thus, left on our own, we do the wrong things. We commit fornication and adultery. (Be honest—how many of you waited till you got married before you had sex?) Left to our own plans, we think of reasons to rob God of our tithes. We steal hours that should be spent working for our employers. When faced with "unwanted" pregnancies, we opt for abortion. If someone hurts our feelings, we harbor resentment instead of extending forgiveness. If we hear of some juicy scandal, we can't help but gossip about it. Then, there is drug addiction, alcohol abuse, pornography, overeating…the list goes on. The flesh is weak, indeed.

I bring up this point not to condemn you but to emphasize how selfish we are because of our weak flesh. Of course, we are good at spotting weaknesses in others, but rarely do we acknowledge our own.

I once received an e-mail with the following message: "I love your Internet site, with all the articles and TV shows, but I challenge you, Brother Tom, to offer your books free of charge."

I wrote back to the sender, saying, "I have another idea. Why don't you tell your boss that you will work for free?"

I haven't heard from him since. We love to think we are superior to others, but, in reality, we are just as weak as they are. This is why everyone must first learn to pray the prayer of submission in order to strengthen his prayer life and make it more effective.

Acknowledge and Repent of Disobedience

Jonah got himself into a whale of a mess. Like Jonah, you, too, may find yourself in a huge mess, whether your marriage is crumbling, your children are out of control, your finances are a bust, your body is sick, or your mind is confused. Imagine the deepest pit, and you'll get a sense of how Jonah must have felt. To make matters worse, he had only himself to blame for his position. Disobedience was the reason he found himself in the belly of a fish. Disobedience is costly! You can claim God's promises, rebuke the devil, and try to pray the prayer of faith, but no prayer will work until you have prayed the prayer of submission.

This is the prayer Jonah prayed in the belly of the fish: *"But I, with a song of thanksgiving, will sacrifice to you. What I have vowed I will make good"* (Jonah 2:9). Once God had heard his prayer, the fish *"vomited Jonah onto dry land"* (Jonah 2:10). The prayer of submission will get you where you need to go.

God gave us His Word—the Bible—as a road map to navigate the winding path of life. Oftentimes, however, we find ourselves drifting off course because we fail to read the directions. It's like trying to assemble a piece of furniture without reading the instructions. It will take longer, and you will probably end up having to dismantle your work and start all over again. Is that how your life feels? Does it seem like you are trying to build your life, only to have it come crashing down, so that you have to begin again? Try consulting the divine road map—the Bible! There is no point in attempting the prayer of faith or the prayer of petition until you have prayed the prayer of submission. Everything begins there!

Submit to the Lord above All Else

Beto joined our church when our congregation was very small. He'd been saved while serving time in prison, and he'd been ordained in the ministry. He had moved to El Paso to do some mission work across the border in Mexico. He and his wife offered to serve us in any way they could. We enjoyed their company and often had dinner with them. During one of our visits, Beto handed me a hundred dollars and told me that God had instructed him to give us this money for personal use, not for ministry. We thanked him for his gift.

A week later, I received a call from Beto. He screamed hysterically, "Pastor Brown, come to our house right now and cast out the devil from my wife!"

I assured him that we would be there as soon as possible. Then, I told Sonia that we needed to visit Beto and his wife.

As I reached for my keys, the Lord spoke to me and said, *Tom, take the hundred dollars with you.*

"Why?" I asked.

After you finish talking to them, Beto will ask for the money back. Give it back to him as a sign.

I put the hundred dollars in my pocket.

When we arrived at the house, Beto was pacing back and forth, shouting at the top of his lungs, "Cast out the devil from my wife!"

I tried to calm him. "What's wrong, Beto? Why do you think your wife needs deliverance?"

"Because she won't obey me! She won't listen to anything I tell her!"

I turned to his wife. "What's going on?"

She explained that Beto wanted her to sign a bank loan for a big purchase. He had a poor credit history and needed her higher score to secure the loan. "I don't think this purchase is wise," she added. "We do not have the money to make the payments."

Beto interrupted her, "It doesn't matter if we have the money or not; God said you must obey your husband. Do what I tell you to do, or else!"

"Or else what, Beto?" she asked.

He clenched his fist. "So help me, I'll put you in the hospital."

I reached out a hand to stop him and said, "Beto, you can't threaten your wife like that. Now, let's reason together about this."

"I don't want any discussion on this. I want my wife to sign the loan, period!" He continued his ranting and raving.

I tried my best to calm Beto, but he said, "Pastor, either you believe in wives obeying their husbands or you don't. Tell my wife she must obey."

"Beto, I can't just tell your wife she must sign her name on something without considering the wisdom of the purchase."

"Ah, so you don't believe in submission. Well, I don't want to go to a church that doesn't tell wives to obey their husbands in everything." Then, he looked at me angrily and added, "Pastor, I want you to give me back the hundred dollars I gave you."

As I reached into my front pocket and pulled out the money he had given me, I said, "Beto, God spoke to me and told me you would ask for this money back, because your heart is hard. Here is the money you gave us. This money will serve as a sign to you of your disobedience to God." We never saw Beto or his wife again.

Beto's wife did not need someone to pray a prayer of deliverance for her; rather, it was Beto who needed prayer—he needed to pray the prayer of submission.

You may be in the same position as Beto, thinking you need this prayer or that prayer, this money or that money; meanwhile, what you really need is to *submit* to the Lord. Why don't you do it right now? Kneel down, bow your head, and confess your disobedience to the Lord. Tell Him that you are ready to obey Him. Once you have prayed the prayer of submission with a sincere heart, you will find the strength to obey God.

Chapter 2

The Prayer of Faith

*Is any one of you sick? He should call the elders of the church to
pray over him and anoint him with oil in the name of the Lord.
And the prayer offered in faith will make the sick person well;
the Lord will raise him up.*
—James 5:14–15

The church has not taken the above passage seriously, especially in regard to divine healing. There is no doubt that healing is a great physical need. Many people spend their life savings on procedures and prescriptions they hope will make them well. Yet the church has not taken this promise at face value. It's simple, really: if we pray the prayer of faith, the sick will get well. There are no ifs, ands, or buts about it. The prayer of faith *will* make the sick person well.

This brings us to an important discussion concerning healing: Does God promise to heal or not? If He does, then you do not need to doubt. Yet there are a great many sincere believers who doubt God's promise to heal. They believe that God *can* heal—that He has the power to do so—but they are unsure whether He has actually promised to heal us. If you are unsure that God promised healing, then you can't have any real faith when you are praying for health.

"Now faith is being sure of what we hope for and certain of what we do not see" (Hebrews 11:1). Faith is always being *"sure"* and *"certain"* of what you hope for yet do not see. Faith has no uncertainty. Faith is always confident.

James made it clear that when you pray, you must believe and not doubt; otherwise, you will receive nothing from God.

> *But when he asks, he must believe and not doubt, because he who doubts is like a wave of the sea, blown and tossed by the wind. That man should not think he will receive anything from the Lord.* (James 1:6–7)

Discovering God's Will

The only way to be sure that your prayers will be answered is to know the will of God.

> *This is the confidence we have in approaching God: that if we ask anything according to his will, he hears us. And if we know that he hears us—whatever we ask—we know that we have what we asked of him.* (1 John 5:14–15)

Many Bible expositors have misread this passage and claimed that it is not possible to know the will of God. Their position is that you should simply say, "God's will be done." However, this is not what the passage is teaching. John began by writing, *"This is the confidence we have in approaching God."* He was dealing with *"confidence."* Any other interpretation imparts a lack of confidence.

John was simply making an obvious point: if you pray according to God's will, you can have confidence that your prayers will be answered. Confidence is built on knowing the will of

God. To show that it is possible to know the will of God, he said, *"And if we know that he hears us…we know that we have what we asked of him."* Thus, you are able to *"know that he hears [you],"* and, as a result, you *"know that [you] have what [you] asked of him."* Before you can approach God with confidence, you must know, in advance, the will of God for whatever you are asking.

Someone might inquire, "How can I possibly know what God's will is, since He is God and I am not?" It's simple: God's will is the same as His promises. God promises to do only what He wants to do—that which is in accordance with His will. No one compels God to promise you anything, so, once He has promised to do something, you know it is His will to do it.

God's Will Is Revealed in His Promises

Without weakening in his faith, [Abraham] faced the fact that his body was as good as dead—since he was about a hundred years old—and that Sarah's womb was also dead. Yet he did not waver through unbelief regarding the promise of God, but was strengthened in his faith and gave glory to God, being fully persuaded that God had power to do what he had promised.

(Romans 4:19–21)

Abraham was *"fully persuaded"* that his hopes were going to come true. Full persuasion leaves no room for doubt. The thing that caused Abraham to be fully persuaded was *"the promise of God."* He was not fully persuaded because he felt his need was legitimate. He was not fully persuaded because he felt his cause was right. No! He was fully persuaded because of one thing: God had promised him a child. The promise left no room for doubt.

Abraham knew the promise in advance. He did not merely pray for a child and then, when he finally received one, conclude that it must have been God's will to give him the child, after all. That's not how faith works. You have to be *"certain of what you do not see"* (Hebrews 11:1). Certainty precedes seeing. You do not wait to see and then become certain. That is not faith. *"We live by faith, not by sight"* (2 Corinthians 5:7). If seeing something makes you a believer, then you are not really a believer. It's the other way around. Believing will make you a *see-er*. You have to believe in the promise that you do not yet "see." Abraham did just this. He believed before he saw. The ground for his assurance was the promise of God.

The Promise of Salvation

Salvation comes through the prayer of faith. Someone might say, "What do you mean? I thought it was the 'sinner's prayer' that saves people."

The sinner's prayer *is* the prayer of faith. It is based on God's promise to save a sinner if he or she prays and makes Jesus Lord of his or her life. The sinner's prayer is based on Romans 10:8–10:

> *But what does it* [being in right standing with God] *say? "The word is near you; it is in your mouth and in your heart," that is, the word of faith we are proclaiming: that if you confess with your mouth, "Jesus is Lord," and believe in your heart that God raised him from the dead, you will be saved. For it is with your heart that you believe and are justified, and it is with your mouth that you confess and are saved.*

Here is the agreement God makes with every sinner: He will save any sinner who prays, saying, "Jesus is Lord!" This is God's promise. As we have learned, the prayer of faith is based on God's promises, and, since salvation is a promise from God, you can count on God saving you if you pray this prayer:

> Dear God, in Jesus' name, I believe that You raised Jesus from the dead, and I confess that He is my Lord. Amen.

This simple prayer is like a contract you make with God. You fulfill your obligation to make Jesus Lord of your life, and, in return, God promises to save you. That's faith.

There is scarcely a week that goes by that I don't receive e-mails from people who question whether or not they have been saved, even though they accepted Christ as Lord. The problem is that they failed to take God at His word and are instead waiting for some feeling or some sense of holiness to convince them that they are saved. They have allowed the falsehoods of Satan to convince them that they are unworthy of salvation, maybe even that they have committed some unpardonable sin. These people know that Satan is the father of lies, yet they believe his word over God's! As a result, they do not embrace the joy that comes from being confident of their salvation. They may very well be saved, but they do not have the joy and peace that salvation brings.

After you have prayed the prayer of faith, you cannot operate based on your feelings. You must take God at His word and count the prayer as answered immediately. When it comes to God's promises and His fulfillment of them, your feelings are irrelevant.

When I got married, I spoke my vows to Sonia, and she spoke her vows to me. The moment we said those words, we were married. Now, I did not *feel* married. I was waiting for some feeling to come over me to let me know that I was married. And I have been waiting for almost three decades to feel married! If I said to my wife, "You know, Sonia, I've never felt married all these years, so I do not think we are married," she would think I had lost my head.

Unfortunately, this is exactly what happens to many people after they pray the sinner's prayer. They do not *feel* saved because they expect some out-of-this-world feeling to confirm their salvation. They *are* saved—not because they feel different but because God promised it. They will experience the joy and peace of salvation only when they stop depending on their emotions and start trusting in God's eternal promise of salvation.

The Promise of Healing

At the beginning of this chapter, we discussed the prayer of faith to make the sick well. Our confidence in the prayer of faith for healing is based on God's promises of health.

Healing is a benefit of being God's child through salvation. The psalmist made this clear when he wrote, *"Praise the LORD, O my soul, and forget not all his benefits—who forgives all your sins and heals all your diseases"* (Psalm 103:2–3). Again, forgiveness of sins and healing are both *"benefits."* Most evangelicals believe that a sinner should be confident when he prays the "sinner's prayer" for salvation but not when he prays for healing, either for himself or for others. Yet healing is just as much a benefit of salvation as is the forgiveness of sins. The psalmist went so far as to say that *"all your diseases"* are healed by God. No disease is exempted from the Lord's healing power! From Scripture, we have sufficient grounds to expect that *all* our diseases will be healed. If not, then how can you expect "*all your sins*" to be forgiven?

The word used for "*benefits*" in this psalm is the legal term for the blessings that "beneficiaries" receive because of a covenant. In other words, these are blessings due to people because of a legal agreement God made with them. Forgiveness and healing are part of the inheritance legally due to the children of God. This means that God agrees, in advance, that He will forgive and heal us. There is no doubt of God's agreement to do these things. We have confidence that these blessings are our inheritance. They are benefits that belong to us, the beneficiaries. This means that the covenant that was established at the cross also included the blessing of health and healing.

The basis of our forgiveness and healing alike is the cross. Most believers are familiar with the Scripture passages that talk about our sins being laid upon Christ, but they forget that our diseases were laid upon Him at the same time: "*He took up our infirmities and carried our diseases*" (Matthew 8:17). Matthew, by the inspiration of the Holy Spirit, quoted from the great atonement chapter in Isaiah—chapter 53—and showed that all healing is based on the simple fact that Christ "*took up our infirmities and carried our diseases.*" Since He took away your infirmities in the same way He took away your sins, you can pray with confidence that God will heal you.[1]

The Promise of the Holy Spirit

Another great blessing we may claim is the gift of the Holy Spirit.

---

1. For a fuller explanation of healing through the atonement, consult my book *Breaking Curses, Experiencing Healing* (New Kensington, PA: Whitaker House, 2011).

Peter replied, "Repent and be baptized, every one of you, in the name of Jesus Christ for the forgiveness of your sins. And you will receive the gift of the Holy Spirit. The promise is for you and your children and for all who are far off—for all whom the Lord our God will call."

(Acts 2:38–39)

There is no doubt that *"the gift of the Holy Spirit"* is *"the promise,"* and that this promise is *"for you and your children and for all who are far off."*

Yes, the Holy Spirit is *"the promise."* Since God promised us the Holy Spirit, no one should ever doubt that he or she can pray in faith for the gift of the Holy Spirit. The Holy Spirit is the most important gift God has given us, and to live without that gift is a tragedy. This gift is so paramount that the Lord, in His teaching on prayer, told us to ask specifically for the Holy Spirit:

Which of you fathers, if your son asks for a fish, will give him a snake instead? Or if he asks for an egg, will give him a scorpion? If you then, though you are evil, know how to give good gifts to your children, how much more will your Father in heaven give the Holy Spirit to those who ask him! (Luke 11:11–13)

Many of God's children are reluctant to ask for the Holy Spirit. Sometimes, they are reluctant because they think they already received the Spirit when they were first saved. While the Holy Spirit definitely comes to live within us at the event of salvation, there is a special gift the Father wants to give His children.

Gordon-John attended a conservative Bible school before landing a job with the El Paso Ballet Company. He looked for a church and ultimately joined our congregation, drawn as he was to our commitment to the Word of God and our friendliness. However, he had an issue with one subject: the baptism in the Holy Spirit.

In his Bible college, he had been told that when you are saved, you are automatically baptized in the Spirit, so there is no other special gift to receive after salvation. Gordon-John was conflicted and would argue over and over with me that he had already been baptized in the Spirit—thus, there was no need for him to pray and ask the Father for it again. I proceeded to show him the many places in Scripture that mention two baptisms: a water baptism, which relates to our salvation, and a baptism in the Spirit, which relates to the power we need in order to be effective witnesses for Christ. Gordon-John took those Scriptures home and began to study the Word for himself.

A few days later, just minutes before we were to begin a Bible study, he walked up to me and said, "Lay hands on me, Pastor Tom. I see in the Word there is a gift my Father wants to give me, and I am ready to receive the Holy Spirit." I laid hands on him. Instantly, he began to speak in tongues, just as I had done when I was baptized in the Spirit. Once he received the Holy Spirit, his eyes were opened to the many blessings God had given him that he had been unaware of before. This is one of the great blessings the Holy Spirit will give you: He will reveal all that Christ wants to give you.

Gordon-John eventually went to the Rhema Bible Training Center to learn more about Spirit-led ministry. Then, he returned to his home country of Malta, where he started a church with his wife, Mariella. Although their church is young, it is now the largest charismatic church in the country, as well as one of the largest evangelical churches there. He attributes his success to his having received the gift of the Holy Spirit.

The other reason some people are reluctant to receive the Holy Spirit is that they are frightened of the supernatural. Isn't it interesting that Jesus compared the idea of asking the Father for the Holy Spirit to asking a natural father for an egg, with the assurance that we would not receive a scorpion instead? Who would ever expect to receive something as frightening as a scorpion from his father if he had asked him for an egg? Jesus was assuaging our fears by assuring us that there is nothing to fear in asking the Father for the Holy Spirit.

Yes, you will receive the supernatural abilities you need, but these abilities are good and not evil. It is *good* to speak in tongues, to heal the sick, and to prophesy. Don't let those gifts scare you. It may be daunting to think that God can give you these mighty abilities, but you need not be afraid of them.

The other thing worth mentioning is that you must not doubt when you ask God the Father for the Holy Spirit. Don't proceed based on your feelings. If you pray for healing but still feel some symptoms, you would not begin to doubt the fact that, according to Jesus, you have already been healed. No, you must claim you have the healing, even if the symptoms persist. So it is with the Holy Spirit: you must believe that you have the Holy Spirit once you ask the Father for this gift, even if you do not see any immediate indicators. Some people get discouraged because they hear about someone like my friend Gordon-John, who spoke in tongues right away, and they wonder why they aren't able to speak in tongues immediately. If you have yet to experience a manifestation of your gift, don't let it bother you. Although I always encourage people to expect to speak in tongues, it is often necessary to believe, in faith, that you have the gift of the Holy Spirit before the gift of tongues manifests.

When Bonnie was a new member of our church, she came forward to receive the gift of the Holy Spirit and was disappointed that she did not speak in tongues. I told her, "Bonnie, believe you have received the gift. You must believe before you have any evidence. Since you asked the Father for the Holy Spirit, He has given Him to you. Thank God, now, for all the manifestations of the Holy Spirit. Say, 'Lord, I want to thank You for giving me the Holy Spirit at church during the Sunday service. I thank You for the gift of tongues.'"

Bonnie thanked God for the gift of the Holy Spirit nearly every day. Then, one day, while she was vacuuming, she began to speak in tongues. Tears streamed down her face at the faithfulness of God. Sometimes, you have to believe you have received what you asked for, like Bonnie did, before there is any physical evidence. Don't allow doubt to rob you of what God has promised.

Chapter 3

The Prayer of Petition

Do not be anxious about anything, but in everything, by prayer and petition, with thanksgiving, present your requests to God. And the peace of God, which transcends all understanding, will guard your hearts and your minds in Christ Jesus.
—Philippians 4:6–7

For a long time, I never knew the difference between the prayer of faith and the prayer of petition. I probably assumed that they were the same. But there are several significant differences between the two.

Principles of Petitioning

To make a petition means to submit a formal request. In my city, I helped spearhead a petition to roll back our city council's decision to provide health benefits for unmarried and same-sex partners of city employees. In a petition, you use simple legal language to express your request. Since it is a request, there is no guarantee that it will be granted. In fact, the first petition that our family-minded group put forth was rejected by the city council. So, we put the second petition before the voters of El Paso. They passed it by an overwhelming majority of votes.

The Outcome Is Never Guaranteed

The first thing you must recognize about a petition to God is that He is not obligated to grant your request. In this way, a petition differs from the prayer of faith, which counts on an affirmative answer because of something God has promised. In a petition, you ask God to do something that He has not specifically said He would do. However, you count on the wisdom, generosity, and love of God to respond to your request as He sees fit. You know how much He cares for you, so you ask Him for something based on His compassion and wisdom. Since it is a "request," it may be denied. However, God will never act in a way that contradicts His promises. He is ever faithful to fulfill them.

A petition to God, therefore, is a humble request. When you make a petition, you do not stand on His promises but on a calm confidence that He will grant your request if it is in your best interest. At the same time, if God does not grant the request, you must not falsely assume that He does not care for you. He may have something even better in store for you.

Let me give you an example. God promises to meet all your needs, and a common way of having one's needs met is by working a job. Let's say that you hear a local department store is hiring, so you submit your application and ask God to give you the job for which you are applying. It is true that God has promised to meet your every need; however, you have no way of knowing that He wants to do so with this particular job at the department store. Suppose He knows that there is a better job available for you. Would you really want God to give you the job at the department store for which you petitioned? Of course not. You want the best job available—one that will bring you fulfillment and earn you the most money.

So, while you may ask God for the department store job, you will not be disappointed if you do not get it—you'll simply trust that God has something better for you.

Petition Does Not Give the Power of Manipulation

You cannot "claim" by faith that a job is yours, because there is no promise from God that He will give you a specific job. Sometimes, people mistakenly use the principles of the prayer of faith in areas where the prayer of petition is better suited. This is especially true in the area of finding a spouse.

Many people who have been single for a while, praying for years that God would give them a godly spouse, become desperate, so that, when someone comes along who fits the criteria they have in mind, they begin "claiming" him or her as a future spouse.

This reminds me of a story I heard. A woman spots a man on the subway and says to him, "You look like my fourth husband."

The man is taken aback. "Woman," he asks, "how many times have you been married?"

She bats her eyelashes at him. "Three times."

God knows that you want to get married. And He wants to give you the desires of your heart. At the same time, you cannot go around claiming people as your spouse. You can petition God to give you a spouse—you may even pray specifically about a particular person—but you cannot claim that person by faith. If you do, you are treating him or her as an object to be owned. Instead, you must understand that each person has the right to choose whom to marry, and you cannot control anyone else's will.

Christopher stumbled upon my Internet site in the course of a search on how to get prayers answered. After reading one of my articles, he was convinced that he had the secret to getting his ex-girlfriend to reconcile with him. He even wrote to me and asked me to pray that this woman would return to him.

I had to explain to Christopher that prayer doesn't work this way. He became upset that I would not agree with him in prayer. I told him that God knows he wants to marry this woman but that he cannot manipulate other people through prayer. The way some people pray, they might as well get a voodoo doll and stick pins and needles through it, because they are trying to force their wills onto other people.

After You Have Petitioned...

The prayer of petition is the way to pray for any legitimate need or desire that God has not specifically promised to give you. You present your request to God, knowing that He is benevolent and wise. If it seems that God has not been benevolent, you can rest assured that He is wise.

Trust God—He Knows Best

God knows when the thing for which you are asking Him is not in your best interest. He always gives what is best—not the second-best desires we come up with.

Charles Neiman tells a funny story about his teenage years. He desperately wanted a Corvette, and he pleaded over and over with his dad to give him the coveted car.

His dad responded, "Son, I love you too much to give you a Corvette."

Yet his words did not compute in the mind of a teen. *If my dad loved me, then he would make me happy by giving me a Corvette*, young Charles reasoned.

Again he pleaded, and this time, his dad said, "Son, the reason I will not buy you a Corvette is because you are not mature enough to handle the speed. I know you, son—you will break every speed limit to test the limits of the car. Then, one day, I will find your Corvette wrapped around a telephone pole."

Charles argued that he would obey the laws. But, even with his slow car, he found a way to accumulate speeding tickets. If he had gotten the Corvette, he very likely would have hurt others or himself. He learned that his dad, in love, had said no for his good.

You have to understand that God, in His infinite love and wisdom, knows if and when you are not ready for the blessing you are asking for. In time, you will be more mature to handle your desires.

Rest in His Peace

The first answer God gives you when you pray the prayer of petition is peace of mind. *"And the peace of God, which transcends all understanding, will guard your hearts and your minds in Christ Jesus"* (Philippians 4:7). I have felt the peace Paul described, time and again. Even if I did not have a firm foundation for my prayer of petition, I still knew that God would either answer my prayer directly or bring about a better answer. In either case, I knew I was within the will of God. Only good was going to come to me.

Let me illustrate the difference between the prayer of faith and the prayer of petition with a sports analogy. I am a season ticket holder for the Dallas Cowboys football team. My ticket guarantees me entrance to every home game. I never have to wonder whether my ticket will get me into a game; I know it will work. I have no reason to doubt it. In this analogy, the confidence with which I approach the gates of the stadium is similar to the prayer of faith. My ticket is a guarantee of God's promises to heal me, save me, and meet all my needs. Thus, praying the prayer of faith is akin to being a season ticket holder: you can be confident that they'll "let you in"—that every prayer that is based on God's promises will get you the promised result.

Now, here is a caveat that illustrates the difference between the prayer of faith and the prayer of petition. My ticket may guarantee me entrance into the stadium, but it does not guarantee that the Cowboys will win the game.

Do you see the difference? God promises to meet all your needs, but He offers no guarantee as to *how* He will go about it. A prayer of petition takes you further than the promises of God in that you do not ask God to go against His promises—that would be foolish and futile—but you specify a way in which you desire God to bless you and your loved ones. Yet you have no guarantee that your request will be fulfilled in the way you have specified. Even so, you leave the results to God, trusting Him completely and experiencing His peace as a result. Peace is the only guarantee of every prayer of petition.

However, you will miss out on the peace of God if you fail to appreciate His wisdom, especially if your prayer is not answered or if the answer is different from how you hoped it would be. If you lack appreciation for God's wisdom, you will be prone to fretting and worrying over your needs and desires. You will lose peace. You might even lose sleep. And you might become angry or indignant, thinking that God has not helped you in the way you thought He should.

A lack of peace always follows a failure to recognize the wisdom of God as superior to your own wisdom—a failure to acknowledge that He knows best.

Even if...

+ you did not get the promotion you prayed for,

+ you did not get accepted to your top choice of universities,

+ that cute girl turned down your invitation to the prom,

+ your boyfriend didn't propose to you after all,

+ you did not win the contest,

+ the project you bid on was assigned to someone else,

+ you didn't get the house you wanted,

+ you were passed over for the lead role in the play,

+ your bald spot did not disappear,

+ you did not sell that item at the price you had set, or

+ the Cowboys did not win...

...you can say, "So what?" Why? Because you have the peace that surpasses all understanding. You may think it would have been great to have your petition granted, but God did not agree, or He would have granted it. Yet you are comfortable trusting His wisdom.

Reorienting the Desires of Your Heart

David wrote, *"Delight yourself in the LORD and he will give you the desires of your heart"* (Psalm 37:4). The desires of your heart are not necessarily based on a specific promise from

God. You may simply want something—a part in a play, a call to preach the Word, a publisher to pick up your manuscript and turn it into a book, and so forth. Each of us has many different desires. What is beautiful about the passage above is that God promises to give us the desires of our hearts, as long as we delight ourselves in Him. That's the secret.

If it seems that God is not rewarding our desires, it's because we are not really *delighting* ourselves in Him. We have more delight in our desires than we do in worshipping Him. I often meet people who have ambitious desires yet seem frustrated because their dreams are not coming true. More often than not, the reason is that they do not delight in the Lord as they should.

Unfortunately, for some people, delighting in the Lord takes a backseat to delighting in their own desires. They try everything to make those desires come true, but, ultimately, they never find true fulfillment.

Notice that Psalm 37:4 does not say that you should "do the right thing"; it says you should "*delight yourself*" in the Lord. Delight refers to your inner desires. It refers to your tastes, your preferences. Delight in reading the Word. Delight in going to church. Delight in praising, worshipping, and serving God. It is not enough to serve God; you must *delight* in serving Him. You must have a proper attitude in service to God. You can't simply drag yourself to church and do your best to stay awake for the duration of the sermon. You should have a spring in your step and a song in your heart as you enter the church. During the message, you should be on the edge of your seat, paying attention and taking notes. In other words, you should take joy in the Lord rather than viewing Him as a burden. When you truly have the joy of the

Lord, you will find greater pleasure in serving Him than you will in the fulfillment of even the most ambitious desires of your own heart.

There is a practical reason for delighting in the Lord. When you delight in the Lord, it changes your desires so that they conform more closely to God's desires, which include His perfect will for your life. You see, many of your desires do not come from the heart but from the flesh. And their origin matters, as we will see. The desires of the heart are spiritual, while the desires of the flesh are carnal.

Discern the Origin of Your Heart's Desires

How do you know if your desires are spiritual or fleshly? The best way is to delight in the Lord, who will filter out from your flesh any desires that are not in line with His will, replacing them with the desires He wants you to have. So, when David said that God *"will give you the desires of your heart,"* he may have meant that as you delight in the Lord, God will place the proper desires within you. Those desires may include the desire to become a pastor, to start a business, to propose to a certain woman, and so forth. When these desires come from the Lord, they are not carnal but spiritual—from the heart.

Some people accuse me of being overly ambitious. They question my motives, saying such things as, "You probably write books to make money," "You are on TV to become famous," and "You pastor a large church to feel powerful." While these accusations sound legitimate, I feel that the desires to pastor, to preach the Word on television, and to write books all sprang from my practice of delighting myself in the Lord—and that He planted those desires within my heart. I definitely feel a desire to do these things, but I am convinced that the root of these desires is a heart that has been born again rather than unregenerate flesh.

When I was young, I wanted to be a professional football player. I was one of the better athletes in my school, despite my small size. But I realized that, unless I got taller, I would never make it as a professional athlete. So, I prayed for God to make me taller. I did not pray this just once in a while; it became my obsession. I wanted so desperately to become taller and play pro football. However, the more time I spent with the Lord, the more my desire to become taller faded away, replaced gradually by a desire to preach the Word.

Did God grant my request to grow taller? No. I am still short. But He replaced that desire with another desire—one of His choosing. I no longer care that I am short. I care that I am anointed. That has become my passion. I know now that God did not grant my request to grow taller because it was not part of His plan for my life. Instead, He planted within my heart a godly desire to teach the Word. This does not mean that I was wrong to pray for God to make me taller. Remember, we are to take every request to God. (See Philippians 4:6.) He is not angered over any prayers that come from a pure heart. I encourage you to pray for your desires to be fulfilled, whatever they may be. At the same time, I encourage you with even greater urgency to draw closer to God so that He can work more effectively on your heart and your desires.

Assess Your Motives

> *You do not have, because you do not ask God. When you ask, you do not receive, because you ask with wrong motives, that you may spend what you get on your pleasures.* (James 4:2–3)

This passage makes two important points: first, you fail to receive from God when you do not ask Him. There are various reasons why you do not ask. Maybe you are too embarrassed. Maybe you think your request is not important to Him. Or, perhaps you do not think He would actually grant you what you want. Whatever the reason, you do not ask God for what you want, and so you never receive it.

The second point is even more important: you fail to receive from God when you ask with wrong motives. Your motives are the inner compulsions that move you. God cares about why you want something. Even if you are asking God to grow your ministry, unless your motives are correct, you will not receive what you want. If your goal is to make more money, gain power and prestige, prove something to others, and the like, your motives are not pure.

God cares deeply about your motives. He wants you to be motivated by a desire to please Him and to serve others. If this is your motivation, God will withhold nothing from you; *"He will make your righteousness shine like the dawn, the justice of your cause like the noonday sun"* (Psalm 37:6). It is easier to see at dawn than at night. However, the best light for seeing is at noonday. This is the way it works with us: at first, we think a particular desire is good, so we ask God for it. Then, as the day wears on and the sun moves directly over us, we are able to see more clearly; perhaps we begin to recognize a wrong motive. The justice of our cause is made clearer to us. We see better than we did in the beginning.

David wrote, *"Be still before the LORD and wait patiently for him"* (Psalm 37:7). Do not become overly concerned if you prayed a prayer that has not yet been answered. Instead, wait patiently for the Lord to either answer your prayer or show you something better.

Chapter 4

The Prayer of Agreement

*If two of you on earth agree about anything you ask for, it will
be done for you by my Father in heaven. For where two or three
come together in my name, there am I with them.*
—Matthew 18:19–20

At a wedding reception, a woman said, "Pastor, let me introduce you to my husband. He has suffered from constant migraines, and I have heard about your ministry of healing. Could you pray for him?"

I looked at the man. "Would you like me to pray for you?"

Surprisingly, he said, "I don't need anyone else to pray for me. God listens to me."

What he said was a half-truth. Of course, God listens to the prayers of His children. Every believer has equal standing with God, who shows no partiality when it come to hearing our prayers. This is what the woman's husband had in mind when he said that he didn't need me to pray for him. He didn't think that my prayers would be more effective than any prayers he had already prayed. And he was right. However, he clearly underestimated the power of praying with other believers for the same thing.

Jesus said, *"If two of you on earth agree about anything you ask for, it will be done for you by my Father in heaven. For where two or three come together in my name, there am I with them"* (Matthew 18:19–20). If Jesus did not expect us to pray together, then He would not have given us this special promise. Certainly, Jesus modeled individual prayer, but He also gave us a special promise that if two or more people pray about something, it will be granted by the Father.

There is a power in corporate prayer that is not found in individual prayer. Look at these additional verses from God's Word as proof:

> *How could one man chase a thousand, or two put ten thousand to flight, unless their Rock had sold them, unless the LORD had given them up?*
> (Deuteronomy 32:30)

> *Five of you will chase a hundred, and a hundred of you will chase ten thousand, and your enemies will fall by the sword before you.* (Leviticus 26:8)

Notice in the verse from Deuteronomy that one man can chase a thousand, but two men working together can put ten thousand to flight. If they are separated, working apart from each other, then they are able to put two thousand to flight; but when they come together, they increase each other's effectiveness fivefold.

This increase of power is called *synergy*. It occurs when two or more agents work together, producing a result that would not have been obtainable by any of them independently. In the field of chemistry, synergy refers to the interaction of substances, such as drugs, that enhances or magnifies the effects of one or more of the drugs. Researchers have discovered that by combining certain drugs, they can accomplish effects that would not have occurred if the drugs were taken on their own. In the realm of business, synergy results when, for example, multiple companies join together and produce results more efficiently than they would have if they had continued as separate entities.

We recognize synergy at work in chemistry and business but often fail to see its application to prayer. The man at the wedding failed to recognize that there was greater power available to us if we joined together in prayer.

Prayer like a Symphony

In Matthew 18:19, the Greek word for *"agree"* is *symphoneo*, from which we take our word *symphony*. In a symphony, dozens of musicians play a variety of musical instruments. When they are warming up, everyone plays independent of everyone else, fine-tuning his or her own instrument. The sound is cacophonous because the notes are not synchronized. But then, when the conductor lifts his baton, all eyes focus on him, and he leads the entire ensemble in a musical piece they play together, in sync. And the effect is breathtaking.

When we pray as "lone rangers," playing our own tune and petitioning for our own needs, I fear that we often may sound strident to God. But when we synchronize our songs and pray together with one voice, it sounds to God like a beautiful symphony—one that prompts a response from heaven. This symphony is achieved by our corporate prayers, not by solitary ones.

An atomic bomb is powerful because of the chain reaction catalyzed by the nuclear fission of atoms. On their own, the atoms are not powerful, but, when fused together, they produce a reaction that results in the release of tremendous amounts of energy. In the same way, our power in prayer increases exponentially when we join with other believers and agree together in prayer.

This principle was embraced by the early church, where *"they all joined together constantly in prayer, along with the women and Mary the mother of Jesus, and with his brothers"* (Acts 1:14). It should not surprise us that God filled the believers with His Holy Spirit, considering the atmosphere of unity they promoted. They prayed in one accord and, as a result, received power from on high. It is also important to note that God filled them with the Spirit *"when the day of Pentecost came,* [and] *they were all together in one place"* (Acts 2:1). God did not fill them separately, individually, or in different locations. He filled them all together in one place. Prior to this, Jesus had said to them, *"But you will receive power when the Holy Spirit comes on you"* (Acts 1:8). The Greek word for *"power"* is *dunamis,* which means "dynamite power"—explosive power. When believers unite in prayer, God comes on the scene and works His miraculous power.

The greatest miracles I have witnessed have occurred while I was praying together with others. Although I have seen God work when I have prayed alone, there is always more power when others join me in prayer. I love united prayer, and so does God.

Corporate Prayer Increases Wisdom

How good and pleasant it is when brothers live together in unity! It is like precious oil poured on the head, running down on the beard, running down on Aaron's beard, down upon the collar of his robes.

(Psalm 133:1–2)

The anointing of the Holy Spirit, as depicted in the oil, started at Aaron's head and ran down his neck. Aaron was the spiritual leader—the high priest—of Israel. As such, he had power. And that power increased when *"brothers lived together in unity."* Aaron represented the people of God, and his anointing began with the head, as it should. But it was not until the brothers were dwelling together in unity that the anointing flowed down the collar of his robes. Aaron's entire head was anointed, and the head is the place of intelligence. It is the seat of wisdom. This passage shows us that God grants us wisdom when we pray together with fellow believers.

Sometimes, we may be praying for something that God, in His wisdom, chooses not to give us. But, when we pray with others, God sometimes opens the eyes of someone else to receive insights into His will concerning that particular situation.

One time, I gathered our congregation together to pray about a piece of property we desired. We even did a "Jericho March" around the property, claiming that piece of land for God. After we had prayed, I heard God say, "This is not your property. I have something better for you." I do not think I would have heard God speak to me if I had prayed by myself. So, in obedience to God's voice, I rejected the offer from the property owner. It wasn't long before, God gave us nine acres of prime real estate elsewhere. The value of that property—where our church now sits—has increased twenty-two times in ten years, while the other property has barely appreciated at all. God is good. By praying together with my congregation, I received an anointing of wisdom to make the right choice.

As with Aaron, the anointing ran down my head, and I received the mind of Christ.

Before making any major decision, it is best to pray with others. Don't presume to have all the wisdom you need. Learn to depend on other people in prayer. When we come together, God speaks to us. He is in our midst, in presence and power.

Corporate Prayer Pushes Us to Persevere

The Bible records some individual prayers, but the vast majority of prayers that are included in the Scriptures were corporate prayers. This ought to tell us a lot about how God works among us.

Once, when the Israelites were going into battle, Moses lifted up his hands in prayer, holding the staff of God in his hands. (See Exodus 17:9.) We read that *"as long as Moses held up his hands, the Israelites were winning, but whenever he lowered his hands, the Amalekites were winning"* (Exodus 17:11). When Moses' arms grew tired, they began to droop, and the Israelites suffered for it. So, a solution was found: *"Aaron and Hur held his hands up—one on one side, on one on the other—so that his hands remained steady till sunset"* (Exodus 17:12). The result was victory for the Israelites: *"So Joshua overcame the Amalekite army with the sword"* (Exodus 17:13), all because Moses' hands were lifted up to the Lord. (See Exodus 17:16.)

Like Moses, we, too, are prone to become exhausted when we stand alone in prayer. We often need others to stand with us and even "hold up our hands," so that our strength returns and our confidence is restored. This is what praying together can do for us. *"I want men everywhere to lift up holy hands in prayer"* (1 Timothy 2:8).

Corporate Prayer Activates the Power of Agreement

When George Truett, the famed pastor of First Baptist Church in Dallas, Texas, was fresh out of seminary, one of his earliest assignments was to preach at a revival meeting. After the service, a big man came up to him, Bible in hand, and said, "Brother Truett, do you believe in this Book?"

"Of course," Truett responded.

The man said, "Do you believe every word in this Book?"

Truett said, "I am a Baptist, and we Baptists believe the Bible."

"Do you believe Matthew eighteen, verses nineteen and twenty?"

"Well," Truett replied, "I don't recall what those verses say, but if it's in the Bible, I believe it."

The man opened up the Bible to Matthew 18:19–20, which we have discussed already:

> *If two of you on earth agree about anything you ask for, it will be done for you by my Father in heaven. For where two or three come together in my name, there am I with them.*

Truett read the verses and then said, "Well, brother, of course I believe it."

The man closed his Bible and said, "I am a rancher, and I have been witnessing to my foreman about Christ. I want him to come to the revival meeting so that he and his family can get saved. Can we pray together that he and his family will come tomorrow night so that you can get them saved?"

"Well, of course, my brother," Truett said, despite his hesitation. You see, George Truett had learned a lot in seminary, but he had never learned how to stand boldly on the Word of God. This rancher had opened his eyes to see that the Bible is not for studying but for trusting. They prayed together.

That night, Truett could not sleep. He kept having thoughts of doubt. *What if the foreman doesn't come to the revival tomorrow? What if he shows up but doesn't respond to the altar call?* Then, Truett recognized the source of these thoughts: *They are coming from Satan.* Out loud, he said, "Satan, you are not going to stop the foreman and his family from coming to the revival, and you will not stop any of them from getting saved!"

Those words calmed his fears, and he fell asleep—only to be awakened again with the same doubts in his head. As he'd done before, he rebuked the devil and then fell back asleep.

At the revival service the following night, Truett scanned the crowd. There was no sign of the rancher or his foreman. Once again, negative thoughts from the devil assaulted his mind, saying, *You see? They are not coming to the meeting. Your prayer will not be answered.*

Under his breath, Truett replied, "I told you, Satan, that the foreman and his family will come tonight and get saved." He battled the negative thoughts for a while, until he was invited to the platform and introduced as the speaker. Soon after he started preaching, he saw the rancher enter the church, followed by another man and a family. Truett smiled and began preaching with passion. When he gave an altar call, the foreman and his family came forward and were saved.

Through this experience, Truett discovered the power in the prayer of agreement. Jesus said, *"If two of you on earth agree about **anything** you ask for, it will be done for you by my Father in heaven."* There is no limit to what you can ask! Never underestimate the power in the prayer of agreement. God can do anything when you agree with others in prayer.

Chapter 5

The Prayer of Release

[Cast] the whole of your care [all your anxieties, all your worries, all your concerns, once and for all] on Him, for He cares for you affectionately and cares about you watchfully.
—1 Peter 5:7 AMP

The above verse describes the prayer of release. We often have a hard time letting go of our concerns and releasing them into God's hands. We fool ourselves into thinking that if we hold on to our problems and continue to worry about them, then something is being done about them. But worrying accomplishes nothing. It just wears us out.

Letting Go Is Active, Not Passive

During a church service, a woman bearing many burdens came forward, knelt by the altar, and began to pray loudly, "Oh, dear Jesus, please take my worries from me, or at least take half of them. I think I could bear the rest!"

The minister calmly placed his hands on her and said, "Sister, that is an unscriptural prayer."

She looked bewildered and said, "What's wrong with asking God to take away my worries?"

"It's wrong because God tells us in His Word that we need to *cast* our cares on Him. You are asking Him to remove something that He told you to give to Him."

"Well," she barked, "what am I supposed to do?"

"Cast all your cares on Him because He cares for you."

She looked at him with disgust, then stood up and walked away, muttering, "I can't do that. I guess I've got to keep my burdens."

Through prayer, we ask for something that God alone can do. But it does not exempt us from all responsibility. We have a duty to give our anxieties over to God and quit worrying. God cannot take our worries away from us. It's up to us to give our worries to Him. You can ask God to take away your sickness but not your worries.

When Jesus said, "**Do not worry** *about your life, what you will eat or drink; or about your body, what you will wear*" (Matthew 6:25), He gave us a command to fulfill. He never said that God would stop us from worrying. We have to decide not to worry. It is possible. We have the power to stop worrying, and we do so by casting our anxieties on God.

The reason you have the power to stop worrying is that worry is just another form of doubt. Doubt is a sin, and you can't ask God to make you stop sinning. *You* have to stop it. Stop sinning; stop doubting; stop worrying.

This does not mean that God will not help you to stop worrying—just don't expect Him to do all the work. God knows that you have needs, and He assumes responsibility for meeting those needs because He loves you. That's His job. Your job is to stop worrying and trust Him.

Overcoming Worries and Worldliness

Jesus said,

So do not worry, saying, "What shall we eat?" or "What shall we drink?" or "What shall we wear?" For the pagans run after all these things, and your heavenly Father knows that you need them. But seek first his kingdom and his righteousness, and all these things will be given to you as well.   (Matthew 6:31–33)

Worry and worldliness are often linked together. We worry over things that are not important. Many teenagers worry excessively about the clothes they wear, fearing that their wardrobe is not full of the latest fashions—and forgetting that character is more important than style. Whether it's fashion or another equally worldly concern, we often drive ourselves crazy worrying about such nonsense.

Often, worldly concerns drive people to commit sinful actions—for example, someone worrying about financial lack may decide to embezzle funds from his employer. I'm convinced that if more believers learned to pray the prayer of release, many of the problems plaguing our society would vanish. As it stands, most people are so driven by their worries that they will compromise their morals and values in an effort to ward off their concerns.

The Worldly Concern of Money

A young believer named Claudia was having trouble making ends meet. She received an e-mail from a long-lost cousin, requesting that she send two thousand dollars to him in Mexico City. He told her that he would use the money to make five times as much, at which point he would repay her the $2000, along with an additional $2000 for her trouble. His offer sounded too good to be true, yet it appealed to Claudia. Ignoring her doubts, she wired the money to her cousin in Mexico City. Of course, she never heard from him again, and she eventually learned that she had no cousins in Mexico City, long-lost or not. She realized that her worries, and perhaps a bit of greed, had caused her to throw away a sum she could not afford to lose.

Unfortunately, the pastorate is not exempt when it comes to running after material things and failing to trust God instead. A pastor friend of mine needed money for his struggling church. He got involved in a pyramid scheme, thinking he'd discovered a great way to raise money. Eventually, the scheme collapsed. The pastor was arrested and had to spend a lot of money on his legal defense—more money than he'd made in the scheme, in fact.

Some ministers who are desperate to appear on television will compromise their ethics in their pursuit of money to fund the broadcasts. For example, they make take up an offering ostensibly to benefit needy children, only to use the money they gather to pay for more TV time. Others dedicate inordinate amounts of time on air to raising money rather than teaching, preaching, and praising. I understand the need for an occasional telethon, but to devote more than half of every show to fund-raising efforts exhibits a lack of trust in God's provision.

One famous television minister found himself in the midst of a media crisis. He was accused by the media of not taking time to pray for the people who had made financial contributions accompanied by personal prayer requests. An investigation revealed that the prayer requests had been sent to the bank, along with the financial contributions; the money had been deposited, while the prayer requests had been discarded.

After the truth came out on national television, this ministry suffered a serious financial blow. In desperation, the minister began to focus his broadcasts entirely on getting the viewers to send money. The anointing on his ministry waned, and he eventually lost almost everything, all because of two things: worrying and worldliness.

The Worldly Concern of Busyness

> As Jesus and his disciples were on their way, he came to a village where a woman named Martha opened her home to him. She had a sister called Mary, who sat at the Lord's feet listening to what he said. But Martha was distracted by all the preparations that had to be made. She came to him and asked, "Lord, don't you care that my sister has left me to do the work by myself? Tell her to help me!" (Luke 10:38–40)

Can you identify with Martha? Do you find yourself overwhelmed with obligations—taking the kids to soccer practice; cooking dinner; cleaning the house; attending parties; volunteering; and so forth? It's easy to get caught up in everything that's on your to-do list, just like Martha did. To make matters worse, her sister simply sat there, calmly and peacefully. Why couldn't she at least worry along with Martha?

That's exactly what Martha wanted to know. And here is how Jesus replied: "*Martha, Martha,…you are worried and upset about many things, but only one thing is needed. Mary has chosen what is better, and it will not be taken away from her"* (Luke 10:41–42). Does Jesus' reply anger you? Didn't Jesus realize that if Martha didn't cook, He would have nothing to eat? *He didn't appreciate all the work Martha was doing for Him,* you might say to yourself. *Poor Martha.*

It is time to stop identifying with Martha and to put yourself in Mary's shoes. Mary recognized that the Word of God is the most important thing—certainly more important than any household chore or job. Yes, you need to work, but you also need to devote yourself to the Word of God, putting it first in your life. This is partly what Jesus meant when He said, *"But seek first his kingdom and his righteousness, and all these things will be given to you as well"* (Matthew 6:33). Making God and His kingdom your highest priorities will not cause you to have fewer things; on the contrary, you will have more—more of that which provides lasting fulfillment. More important, when you put God first and give His Word priority, then the possessions you have will not *possess* you. Those who prize material possessions over the Word of God don't really have those things; those things *have* them. God wants you to *own* things—He doesn't want things to own *you.*

Worry is proof that you are owned by your possessions. They keep you up at night. They keep you from serving God. You end up wasting time serving them instead. Worry keeps you in bondage to things.

Break the Habit of Worrying

Jesus told Martha, *"You are worried and upset about many things."* Worry can become a habit—a mind-set that settles in automatically in response to problems and hardships. Worrying may be a harder habit to kick than cigarettes.

However, you don't need a "worry patch" to quit; you just need to realize how much God loves you and learn to trust Him above all else.

*"Casting the whole of your **care**...for He **cares** for you affectionately and **cares** about you watchfully"* (1 Peter 5:7 AMP). There are two different Greek words used for *"care"* in this verse. The first *"care"* refers to your temporary needs and worries, which you are to cast on Jesus. The second *"care,"* used in *"He cares for you"* and *"[He] cares about you,"* conveys a sense of permanence. God is always caring for you, even when you do not realize it. Many people view God as an "all-seeing eye" that does not watch His children with affection. But, the truth is, God is crazy about you. He is madly in love with you.

Think about when you first fell in love. You could not stop thinking about your beloved. He or she was always on your mind. And that's exactly how God feels about you! Only, His love never fades; the "honeymoon" is ongoing. When you experience a revelation of how deeply God loves you, worrying will become an easy habit to break.

Say out loud, "God loves me. He is crazy in love with me. I am always on His mind. He can't stop thinking about me. He is always watching over me."

Do you see how foolish it is to worry? It makes no sense, especially when we have such a loving heavenly Father watching over us.

Cast Your Cares

"Casting the whole of your care..." (1 Peter 5:7 AMP). When you go fishing, you *cast* out your line to catch a fish. Take a

little child fishing, and he'll probably grow impatient, wanting to reel in his line before he's caught anything. But a skilled fisherman knows the importance of being patient. He knows that if he just waits a while, eventually, the fish will bite.

Patiently awaiting a catch is a lot like casting your cares on God. By this process, you give God your anxieties, and, in exchange, He gives you peace and, ultimately, answers. But you must be patient.

Maybe you tried casting your cares to God, only to reel them in again. The verse says to cast your cares *"once and for all."* You need to cast your cares only once. If you keep casting your cares over and over again, it reveals that you are not fully trusting God. Let God take over your life. Let Him supply what you need.

I believe that the more we worry, the longer God takes to answer our prayers. We are like impatient children constantly reeling in the line they cast before any fish have bitten. Those children aren't going to catch anything. When they see the patient fisherman bringing in a big catch, they get mad and blame their bait or their rods. Yet the problem isn't the bait or their rods; it's their impatience. Likewise, your problem may not be your prayer but your impatience.

Quit acting like a little child. Don't cast your cares on God for a few days, only to reel them back in again. Using the prayer of release sends your worries permanently to God, allowing Him to take care of your needs.

Remember That God Will Not Let You Down

Sonia and I were young when we got married. I worked part-time at a fast-food restaurant, and although I didn't make a lot of money, we got to eat plenty of hamburgers. Then, one evening, I received a call from a fellow employee, who told me that the restaurant had closed its doors due to a lack of business.

I said, "They closed the restaurant? Today? So, I don't have a job anymore." Then, I started laughing. My laughter was almost uncontrollable when I hung up the phone.

My new bride was not laughing with me. "What happened, Tom?"

"They closed the restaurant. I'm out of a job. Isn't that funny?"

She was not amused.

I told her, "Don't worry. If God closed this door, He has a better door He will open."

I truly believed that. So, we prayed and committed our finances to His hands.

Later that week, I was hired to work full-time at another company that offered better hours. God had come through again. I can't say I have always acted with as much faith as I exhibited in that instance. Yet I regret every hour I have wasted worrying, because God has never let me down.

Friend, God will never let you down, either. When the devil tries to get you to worry, just laugh, remembering that God has a great plan for you.

When you pray, don't worry.

Chapter 6

The Prayer of Praise

From the lips of children and infants you have ordained praise
because of your enemies, to silence the foe and the avenger.
—Psalm 8:2

Most people do not think that praise is a form of prayer, but it is. Prayer is simply talking to God, and there is no higher form of prayer than praising Him. In praise, you do not mention your needs; you simply tell God how great He is. He likes to hear that—not because He needs His ego stroked but because His children need to remind themselves of how big He is. Praise helps us to realize God's greatness. It also puts us in a position of favor, so that God will meet our needs in a more spectacular way than if we had merely asked Him without praising Him. Praise is the highest expression of faith.

The Power of Praise

The year was 897 B.C., and the situation was hopeless. Although Judah's army was growing larger, it was tiny in comparison with the three nations that had joined together for the express purpose of annihilating them. What was Judah to do under these horrible circumstances? King Jehoshaphat knew the solution.

*After consulting the people, Jehoshaphat appointed men
to sing to the LORD and to praise him for the splendor
of his holiness as they went out at the head of the army,
saying: "Give thanks to the LORD, for his love endures
forever."*   (2 Chronicles 20:21)

Isn't that a strange tactic? Instead of fighting or surrendering, the king, after hearing from God (see 2 Chronicles 20:1–3), decided to position everyone who was skilled in praise on the front lines, for the express task of praising God!

What does praising God have to do with warfare, you ask? Let's consider another Scripture that sheds light on their relationship. *"From the lips of children and infants you have ordained praise because of your enemies, to silence the foe and the avenger"* (Psalm 8:2). Notice that praise shuts the mouth of the enemy. In the case of King Jehoshaphat and Judah, praise cut the enemy's lines of communication and threw them into utter confusion.

*As they began to sing and praise, the LORD set ambushes
against the men of Ammon and Moab and Mount Seir
who were invading Judah, and they were defeated. The
men of Ammon and Moab rose up against the men from
Mount Seir to destroy and annihilate them. After they
finished slaughtering the men from Seir, they helped to
destroy one another.*   (2 Chronicles 20:22–23)

The enemies were befuddled. They couldn't tell the difference between the army of Judah and their own army, and they eventually killed themselves off.

For Judah, a seemingly hopeless situation proved to be a blessing in disguise.

When the men of Judah came to the place that over-looks the desert and looked toward the vast army, they saw only dead bodies lying on the ground; no one had escaped. So Jehoshaphat and his men went to carry off their plunder, and they found among them a great amount of equipment and clothing and also articles of value—more than they could take away. There was so much plunder that it took three days to collect it. On the fourth day they assembled in the Valley of Beracah, where they praised the LORD. This is why it is called the Valley of Beracah to this day. Then, led by Jehoshaphat, all the men of Judah and Jerusalem returned joyfully to Jerusalem, for the LORD had given them cause to rejoice over their enemies. (2 Chronicles 20:24–27)

If the men of Judah had not battled their enemies—in the power of the Lord—they would not have received so much wealth. This battle was God's way to bless Judah. To emphasize the reason for their victory, they named the battle site "*Beracah,*" the Hebrew word for "praise."

Praise Foils the Enemy's Schemes

A similar situation occurred in 1799 on Easter morning in Feldkirch, Austria. The townspeople heard that Napoleon Bonaparte was leading the French army on a campaign to take their city captive. But the local bishop objected to any evacuation plans. He told the people, "This is Easter. We must celebrate the victory of our Lord on this day with praise. I want every church to ring its bells and the citizens to shout for joy throughout the day, reminding everyone of the resurrection."

As they did, Napoleon's generals became confused. They decided not to attack the city, because they assumed the Austrian army had arrived to defend it. The bells never stopped ringing until the French army broke rank and left. Praise gave the Austrian village victory.

Praise Achieves Breakthrough

The apostle Paul also knew the power of praise. While he and Silas were in prison, they began praising God in the midnight hour. Being confined in prison would cause many Christians to adopt a mind-set of defeat, but, instead of whining, these men praised God. Sure, they were battered and bruised; they had just been beaten. Their feet and hands were chained. Yet, they knew without a doubt that God *"gives power to the weak* ["*faint*" KJV]" (Isaiah 40:29 NKJV). Who receives power from God? Those who are weak and about to faint, those who are ready to give up, the discouraged—these people are good candidates for God's power.

And why does God give them His power?

> *But they that wait upon the LORD shall renew their strength; they shall mount up with wings as eagles; they shall run, and not be weary; and they shall walk, and not faint.* (Isaiah 40:31 KJV)

To praise God is to wait on the Lord. And what happens when we praise God? *"Keep silence before me, O islands; and let the people renew their strength"* (Isaiah 41:1 KJV). God shuts the mouths of our enemies and gives us time to renew our strength.

What happened to Paul and Silas as a result of their praising God in prison?

> *And suddenly there was a great earthquake, so that the foundations of the prison were shaken: and immediately*

> *all the doors were opened, and every one's bands were*
> *loosed.* (Acts 16:26 KJV)

Just when it looks like you are stuck in a terrible situation, God suddenly breaks through. I love it when something happens *suddenly*—a breakthrough that only God could have orchestrated in the midst of a situation that seems permanent, where it looks as though nothing will change, despite your prayers and the prayers of others on your behalf.

When these "impossible" situations arise, what should you do? Praise Him through whom *"all things are possible"* (Matthew 19:26; Mark 10:27).

An Expression of Excitement

The common Hebrew word for "praise" is *halal*, from which we get the word *hallelujah*—"to be excited about," "to boast," "to rave," "to celebrate."

Picture a football game at which your team has just scored the winning touchdown. What is your response? Do you react solemnly, with a dignified "That is very nice. I'm glad we won"? No! You yell, you shout, you jump up and down, screaming, "Yea! We won!" You are beside yourself. No one judges you for your jubilant celebration. In fact, everyone else in the stadium whose team won is ecstatic, as well. This is the way you should act! No one acts embarrassed. It's appropriate for the occasion.

Yet, when it comes to church, many believers seem to think that God wants us to remain stoic and dignified, to avoid being overly emotional. Some churchgoers disapprove of any emotional outbursts of praise. They want their services to remain be quiet and reserved. But that is not praise!

How is it that we can jump and holler when our favorite football team scores, but when Jesus triumphs over the devil, we keep our composure? People get saved in the service. People are healed, and still more people are touched and changed. Yet no one is shouting or leaping for joy. How can this be? We have acted this way because we don't have praise in our hearts. Praise must come from the heart. It must be felt. The praise can't be contained. It's appropriate for the occasion.

Manifestations of Praise

Praise is something you do. It always involves action; it's never passive. Some people are wary of "Spirit-filled" churches, saying, for example, "I don't know why those people feel the need to go around dancing and shouting. It isn't necessary. God knows my heart. He understands how much I appreciate Him." Those who say such things have been fooled into thinking that praise is inactive. Yet the Hebrew words for "praise" used in the Bible show praise to be a high-energy physical activity.

Yadah

> *I will give you thanks [yadah] in the great assembly; among throngs of people I will praise you.*
>
> (Psalm 35:18)

Although its shortest definition is "thanks," the word *yadah* also means "to throw, cast." I believe this is partly why people raise their hands in praise and worship—they are "throwing" their praises toward heaven; they are "casting" their worship heavenward. If you have ever attended a rock concert, you probably have witnessed countless adoring fans with hands uplifted. At a sporting event, the spectators may cheer while pumping their fists in the air. From these examples, we understand that God designed us to express excitement and adoration by lifting our hands.

Lifting hands is also a universal sign of surrender. When a police officer is making an arrest, he is likely to say, "Put your hands in the air." He does this to make sure the offender will not do something destructive, such as shooting a gun, to escape arrest.

In the same way, you raise your hands to God to signify a surrender to His lordship. You are promising not to flee from Him. You have finished fighting, and the victory is the Lord's.

Barak

> *Bless [barak] the LORD, O my soul, and forget not all his benefits: who forgiveth all thine iniquities; who healeth all thy diseases; who redeemeth thy life from destruction; who crowneth thee with lovingkindness and tender mercies; who satisfieth thy mouth with good things; so that thy youth is renewed like the eagle's.*
> (Psalm 103:2–5 KJV)

The word *barak* means "to bless," "to cause to kneel." It implies saying something good about someone, just as the above psalm indicates several salient qualities about God as it delineates blessings He bestows on His children. When we bless the Lord, we proclaim the benefits He has given us, such as health, salvation, and deliverance.

Zamar

> *I will be glad and rejoice in you; I will sing praise [zamar] to your name, O Most High.*   (Psalm 9:2)

Zamar means "to sing praise." I'll admit it—I do not have a good singing voice. However, you do not need to be a skilled vocalist to sing to the Lord. He has a way of making our voices sound like the sweetest music to His ears.

Many people who aren't excellent singers still enjoy singing—in the shower, for example, where the acoustics make everyone sound great. I believe God enjoys our singing, even if other people do not. And if singing isn't your thing, you may "sing" a song to the Lord through the use of a musical instrument.

Two major Christian denominations—the Eastern Orthodox Church and the Church of Christ—ban musical instruments in worship. They base their policy on an assertion that musical instruments are not mentioned in the New Testament.

This argument is erroneous. First of all, any command of God from the Old Testament that was not fulfilled or set aside under the new covenant should still be heeded by believers. The Word of God encourages—even commands—us to use instruments to praise God.

> *Praise him with the sounding of the trumpet, praise him with the harp and lyre, praise him with tambourine and dancing, praise him with the strings and flute, praise him with the clash of cymbals, praise him with resounding cymbals. Let everything that has breath praise the* LORD. *Praise the* LORD. (Psalm 150:3–6)

How much clearer can it be? The truth is, the practice of banning musical instruments has more to do with tradition than Scripture, which is clear and forthright in its exhortations to God's people to use musical instruments in their worship of the Lord.

Someone might argue, "Where in the New Testament does it mention musical instruments?" This person is following the "silent theory"—if something is not mentioned specifically in Scripture, he assumes that we should not do it. Yet you cannot argue against the use of instruments based on the Bible's apparent silence on the subject.

For those who feel they require a New Testament verse that substantiates the use of musical instruments, consider Ephesians 5:19: "*Speak to one another with psalms, hymns and spiritual songs. Sing and **make music** in your heart to the Lord.*" What is the difference between psalms and hymns? *Strong's Exhaustive Concordance* defines *psalm* as "a set piece of music, a sacred ode accompanied with the voice, harp or other instruments." The word is taken from the Greek word *psao*, meaning "to rub or touch; to twitch or twang." It was used to describe the work of Jubal, "*the father of all who play the harp and flute*" (Genesis 4:21). The harp made a twanging sound, hence the term *psao*, or "psalm." Since the New Testament encourages the use of psalms, we can conclude that musical instruments are involved.

A hymn, on the other hand, is a song without instruments. Paul and Silas were singing hymns to God while in prison. (See Acts 16:25.) They could not sing psalms because, obviously, they had no instruments in prison.

Machowl

> Let them praise his name with dancing [machowl] and
> make music to him with tambourine and harp.
>
> (Psalm 149:3)

Dancing, especially leaping, is an obvious expression of jubilation. You cannot stand still while you are celebrating.

Let's think again about a football game. When the home team scores a touchdown, the fans leap up and down with excitement. It is natural to move your feet when you are excited.

This is what David did when the ark of the covenant was recovered from the Israelites' enemy. David was filled with excitement, and he danced before the Lord with all his strength.

> As the ark of the LORD was entering the City of David, Michal daughter of Saul watched from a window. And when she saw King David leaping and dancing before the LORD, she despised him in her heart.
>
> (2 Samuel 6:16)

Notice the reaction of David's wife, Michal. She found his display of jubilation to be vulgar and crass. When David arrived home, his wife blurted out, *"How the king of Israel has distinguished himself today, disrobing in the sight of the slave girls of his servants as any vulgar fellow would!"* (2 Samuel 6:20). People who are out of touch, spiritually speaking, cannot appreciate the value of dancing before the Lord. Don't be caught looking down at those who love to dance before the Lord. In fact, go a step further and join them!

If you feel too embarrassed to dance in praise to God, it shows how carnal and self-centered you have become. David told his wife, in effect, "Honey, you haven't seen anything yet. You think I look like a fool in your eyes? Well, I am going to get so wild for the Lord that I will embarrass even myself." (See 2 Samuel 6:21–22.)

Plenty of worldly people go wild with dancing when they've consumed too much alcohol, for example. How much more jubilant should believers be in the way they praise the

Lord? We should let down our hair and be happy to serve Him through dancing, no matter how embarrassed we may feel at first.

Here's something else I have noticed about dancing. In church, when everyone is dancing together in praise, it puts everyone on the same level—doctors, lawyers, CEOs, janitors, and bricklayers. If you cannot dance before the Lord, you need a real release in your Spirit. If you find yourself unable to dance in front of other people at church, try dancing alone, for starters. Free yourself in the Spirit in the privacy of your own house. Then, when you feel more comfortable, let loose in church.

Shabach

> *Shout [shabach] with joy to God, all the earth!*
> (Psalm 66:1)

Shabach means "to commend," "to address in a loud tone," "to praise." Many believers are uncomfortable with "loud" religion. However, I do not know how Christianity can be quiet. It is amazing how the religious have turned Christianity into a subdued practice, when our faith should make us shout with joy. Things like the incarnation, the resurrection, and the falling of the Holy Spirit should elicit a shout of joy from our spirits.

When Jesus healed the ten lepers, whom did He commend? He complimented the one who *"came back, praising God in a loud voice"* (Luke 17:15). This man was so grateful for his health that he could not hold back. He shouted with the voice of victory. If you can shout when your favorite team scores, then you should shout doubly loud when Christ gives you victory.

Towdah

> *He who sacrifices thank [towdah] offerings honors me, and he prepares the way so that I may show him the salvation of God.* (Psalm 50:23)

The Hebrew word *towdah* means "confession, praise, thanksgiving." Praise is often referred to as a sacrifice (see, for example, Hebrews 13:15), and sacrificial praise is the most impressive form of praise. A sacrifice is something given up in thanks and honor, in exchange for something greater.

In baseball, there is a play called a "sacrifice," and it occurs when the team that's up to bat already has a player on base. The batter purposely bunts the ball, or hits it in such a way that he gives himself up for an "out," so that the runner can advance to the next base. The batter is out, but, as a result, his team moves forward and comes closer to scoring a run.

There are times when the last thing you feel like doing is offering thanks and praise to God. How often have you been "down in the dumps" on your way to church? Sometimes your flesh wants to remain seated and silent while the music plays and others around you stand to worship through singing and dancing. You don't feel like praising God; all you want is to be left alone.

It is in those times that you *need* to sacrifice your lips to God and praise Him with all your heart, your mind, your soul, and your strength. For, when you do, God rewards your sacrifice with such blessings as salvation, health, deliverance, and more. When everything else seems to fail—your prayers, your confession of faith, your Bible reading—try praise. Often, praise works when nothing else does. When you've exhausted the other types of prayer but received no answers, it's time to employ the prayer of praise.

Healed through the Power of Praise

Robert survived a horrific automobile accident that would have killed most people. Even so, his back was broken, and two disks had to be surgically removed. Robert couldn't take even one step without the aid of a walker. At a Sunday morning service, he stood during a group prayer for the sick. After I had prayed, many people testified of having been healed. But we weren't finished yet. I felt that we needed to give God praise. So, we sang a few choruses of a worship song. After the music, everyone sat down, except for Robert. His hands were lifted in praise, as tears streamed down his face. I recognized the glory of God all over him.

I walked up to him. Through his tears, he told the congregation, "I felt something click in my back." I took him by the hand and led him just a few steps. In a matter of seconds, he began walking briskly—without my aid. Still crying with joy, he continued to praise God for all His goodness. After the service that day, Robert threw his walker in the back of his pickup truck, and he hasn't used it since. The difference was that when everyone else had finished praising God, Robert continued. And he was healed through the power of praise.

Chapter 7

Prayer in the Spirit

Pray in the Spirit on all occasions
with all kinds of prayers and requests.
—Ephesians 6:18

Paul singled out one type of prayer as particularly important: prayer in the Spirit. Prayer in the Spirit is a unique type of prayer that isn't found in the Old Testament. The reason is that praying in the Spirit was not possible until the day of Pentecost, when the Holy Spirit fell. Prior to Pentecost, the Holy Spirit had not yet come in His fullness. Thus, prayer in the Spirit is for our age.

Prayer in the Spirit is one of the most powerful types of prayer, because, when you pray in the Spirit, the Holy Spirit prays *through* you. *"For if I pray in an [unknown] tongue, my spirit [by the Holy Spirit within me] prays..."* (1 Corinthians 14:14 AMP). Think about it: when you pray in the Spirit, the third person of the Trinity takes over and speaks for you. What better way could there be to pray?

In the same way, the Spirit helps us in our weakness. We do not know what we ought to pray for, but the Spirit himself intercedes for us with groans that words cannot express. And he who searches our hearts knows the mind

> *of the Spirit, because the Spirit intercedes for the saints in accordance with God's will.* (Romans 8:26–27)

In our human weakness, we have only a limited understanding of our needs, as well as the needs of others. How can we know what we should pray for? We trust that the Holy Spirit will give us the words to say. God knows that our prayers are imperfect—often selfish and displaying a limited knowledge of situations. There are many factors that may hinder how we pray and what we ask for in prayer. When we pray in the Spirit, however, these limitations vanish, and we pray the perfect will of God, every time. "*The Spirit intercedes for the saints in accordance with God's will.*"

The Role of Tongues

Many people wonder whether "praying in the Spirit" is the same as "praying in tongues." Some believe that praying in the Spirit involves more gusto and passion than praying in tongues. While I am sure that the Holy Spirit can inspire our prayers and give us passion, I believe praying in tongues and praying in the Spirit to be one and the same. Paul alluded to this when he said, "*The Spirit himself intercedes for us with groans that words cannot express.*" Human words "*cannot express*" what the Spirit is praying. This is when tongues come into play. Tongues are not human words but a divine language. Let me explain the gift of speaking in tongues more fully.

An Experience That Stirs Controversy

Speaking in tongues is one of the most controversial phenomena in Christianity. Pentecostalism and the charismatic movement have brought this practice into the mainstream—in fact, these branches of Christianity have become, without a doubt, the fastest-growing segments of the faith. These movements are impacting the world in ways that go beyond even the Protestant Reformation. Yet, with all the talk about speaking in tongues, few people understand what it's all about. You may be surprised to discover that the Bible mentions speaking in tongues thirty-five times. Clearly, this is not a subject to be treated lightly or cast aside by the church. God included nothing trivial in the pages of His Book.

There are those who do not consider the practice of tongues legitimate, probably because they have never experienced it. Their interpretation of the Bible's references to tongues is colored by a bias that is indisposed to accept the practice. Legendary Bible teacher and healing minister Smith Wigglesworth was once a critic of tongues. He argued with his wife and with other Pentecostal ministers about tongues, insisting that he did not believe in it and that, if it was real, he did not need it. Eventually, he became so hungry for more of God that he was filled with the Spirit and spoke in tongues. He would later tell people, "Before, I had an argument. Now, I have an experience with God." Experience is the best teacher.

I bring this up because many people who have never spoken in tongues talk as though they are experts in this field, when, in reality, their opinions are based on theory alone. Who should know more about tongues: those who speak in tongues or those who don't? Since I am among those who speak in tongues, I feel that I can bring scriptural wisdom combined with practical experience to this chapter. I will attempt to clarify some common misunderstandings and show the importance and benefits of praying in tongues.

An Experience That Edifies

The apostle Paul wrote, "*He who speaks in a tongue edifies himself....I would like every one of you to speak in tongues*" (1 Corinthians 14:4–5). With these positive statements about tongues, why do so few Christians speak in tongues? I believe the reason is a dearth of sound, rational, biblical teaching on the scope and value of speaking in tongues.

A few years ago, I spoke to a group of Mormons at one of their schools and shared my testimony of how God had saved me and filled me with the Holy Spirit, with the evidence of speaking in tongues. After my talk, the students were invited to pose questions, and the most popular topic of their inquiries was speaking in tongues. One student asked, "What does speaking in tongues do for you?"

My answer was this: "It does exactly what the Bible says it does: '*He who speaks in a tongue edifies himself.*'" To "edify" is to build up or "recharge," as you would a battery. Every believer becomes spiritually drained, at times, and needs to be "recharged" by the Holy Spirit. And God designed the practice of speaking in tongues as one way to renew our spirits.

An Experience of Speaking Heaven's Language

Many people describe speaking in tongues as "gibberish" or "nonsense." The truth is, speaking in tongues is the most intelligent, most perfect language in the universe. It is God's language.

Most languages are identified by their place of origin—where they were first spoken, whether a country, a region, or another area—and named accordingly. For example, English comes from England. Spanish comes from Spain. Italian comes from Italy.

What language do you suppose is spoken in heaven? Well, where do tongues come from? Heaven! Everyone in heaven understands the language of tongues and uses it to communicate. As the apostle Paul wrote, *"For anyone who speaks in a tongue does not speak to men but to God. Indeed, no one understands him; he utters mysteries with his spirit"* (1 Corinthians 14:2). Thus, tongues is rightly defined as a heavenly language.

Jesus said that those who believed in Him would *"speak in new tongues"* (Mark 16:17). He was referring to a language no one had ever spoken before. Contrary to bad theology, speaking in tongues is not the God-given ability to preach the gospel in various foreign earthly languages, for how could any extant earthly language be *"new"*? The tongues of men are "old." It is only appropriate that *"new tongues"* be spoken by those of the "new birth." It is natural and normal to speak in the language of your birth. We are born again from above; therefore, we should speak the language from above—the language called *"new tongues."*

An Experience That Depends on the Holy Spirit

The first people to speak in tongues were Jesus' disciples. This occurred on the day of Pentecost. Yet many people assume that the disciples were speaking different human languages, based on the fact that other people from various linguistic backgrounds could understand what they were saying. I believe this conclusion is inaccurate. The miracle that took place on the day of Pentecost was twofold: a miracle of *speaking* and *hearing*.

The first miracle was the speaking in tongues; the second miracle was the enabling of some to understand the tongues.

We know that not everyone understood the tongues, because some onlookers made fun of the disciples and accused them of being drunk. (See Acts 2:13.) This suggests that they could not make out what the disciples were saying. Meanwhile, those who were able to understand the tongues were perplexed, because each one heard only his own native language, not the languages of the other people. (See Acts 2:6.) The Bible tells us that there were over fourteen groups of foreigners present, representing many nations and speaking different languages. (See Acts 2:9–10.) Yet each person heard the disciples praising God in his own language. They exclaimed, *"How is it that each of us hears them in his own native language?"* (Acts 2:8).

The disciples were not preaching the gospel in tongues; rather, they were *"declaring the wonders of God"* (Acts 2:11). They were not speaking to men but to God. (See 1 Corinthians 14:2.) The other people gathered there were simply listening in on their praises to God, and some were able to discern what was being said. It wasn't until Peter stood up to address the crowd in a common language that the gospel was preached. So, we see that speaking in tongues is not a gift given for the purpose of enabling believers to preach the gospel in languages other than their native tongues.

On the day of Pentecost, the disciples were not speaking in human languages; they were speaking in unknown tongues. But God enabled those whose hearts were open to understand what the disciples were saying.

A Precursor to Praying in the Spirit: Baptism in the Holy Spirit

Let us look in greater detail at the first scriptural account of speaking in tongues:

When the day of Pentecost came, they were all together in one place. Suddenly a sound like the blowing of a violent wind came from heaven and filled the whole house where they were sitting. They saw what seemed to be tongues of fire that separated and came to rest on each of them. All of them were filled with the Holy Spirit and began to speak in other tongues as the Spirit enabled them. (Acts 2:1–4)

The above passage recounts an experience that Jesus called the "baptism with the Holy Spirit." It was the fulfillment of Jesus' promise that *"in a few days you will be baptized with the Holy Spirit"* (Acts 1:5). Every Christian believes in water baptism, but few are inclined to accept the better baptism—the baptism in the Holy Spirit.

Many theologians confuse the baptism in the Holy Spirit with salvation (an idea we discussed earlier), regarding these two distinct experiences as being one and the same, and thereby mislead countless believers who fail to realize that this isn't what the Bible teaches. Jesus clearly defined the baptism in the Holy Spirit as a separate experience from salvation that comes after a person has been saved, although it may occur immediately after salvation.

The story of the Samaritan converts in Acts 8:5–25 plainly proves this. Philip preached the gospel to this group of Samaritans, who joyfully accepted Jesus as their Savior and were born again. They confirmed their faith by being baptized in water. Yet, despite their salvation experience and water baptism, Philip called for the apostles to come and pray that they would also receive the Holy Spirit. It is clear from this account that being saved is not the same as receiving the Holy Spirit, even though the Holy Spirit is definitely involved in salvation.

Another biblical account that illustrates this fact is found in Acts 19:1–7. Paul met some of the disciples of John the Baptist. Yet he thought they were believers in the Lord Jesus, because they talked so much about repentance. Knowing that they lacked spiritual power, he asked them, *"Did you receive the Holy Spirit when you believed?"* (Acts 19:2). The question itself proves that Paul, as well as the rest of the early church, believed that it was possible to be a believer in Jesus without having received the Holy Spirit. If receiving the Holy Spirit was automatic at conversion, then why did Paul ask these believers whether they had received the Holy Spirit upon coming to salvation?

The Physical Evidence

I was baptized in the Holy Spirit at the First Assembly of God church here in El Paso, Texas. The preacher invited those who were ready to dedicate themselves to the ministry to come forward for prayer. The first to go forward was a tall, slender fellow named Timmy. I thought, *If Timmy can go forward, I can, too.* So, I followed Timmy to the podium at the front. Without warning, Timmy fell to the floor, as if something had hit him. Seconds later, I felt as if I was being hit by something, and down I went, prostrate on the ground. I began to weep uncontrollably as I sensed God's presence all over me. This went on for several minutes.

The thought occurred to me, *This must be what my church has been talking about all these years. This must be the baptism in the Holy Spirit.* No sooner had I thought this than a Scripture came to mind: *"All of them were filled with the Holy Spirit and began to speak in other tongues"* (Acts 2:4).

If I've been filled with the Holy Spirit, then I'll speak in other tongues, I reasoned in my mind. Right then, I began speaking in other tongues—and I haven't stopped yet! Glory to God!

You see, the physical proof of the baptism in the Holy Spirit is the same as the evidence the disciples had: speaking in tongues. There may be other evidences, as well, but the one evidence that should always manifest is speaking in tongues.

There are five examples in the Bible of people receiving the baptism in the Holy Spirit. (See Acts 2:4; 8:17; 9:17–18; 10:44; 19:6.) In three out of the five examples, we are told that specific signs took place. In the other two examples, the manifestation of physical signs is implied, albeit not mentioned specifically. Yet, based on the other three examples, we can build a solid case regarding what ought to happen when someone is baptized in the Spirit.

We are told in these three examples that certain physical manifestations took place. In each case, more than one physical sign was present, which suggests that there is usually more than one sign taking place when people are baptized in the Holy Spirit. Yet, there is one sign—and only one sign—that is common to all three examples: speaking in tongues. Based on this observation, we can conclude that the standard sign of the baptism in the Holy Spirit is speaking in tongues.

Speaking in tongues is the physical, biblical evidence that one is baptized in the Holy Spirit. We should not settle for anything less than scriptural evidence.

If you have not yet been baptized in the Holy Spirit, seek God in prayer and ask for it in faith. God never leaves a dry soul thirsting. You need this gift if your prayer life is going to be successful. Why not pray the follow prayer and receive the baptism in the Spirit?

> Father, I come to You in the name of Jesus. I believe that You sent the Holy Spirit to the earth on the day of Pentecost and that He is here right now to empower me to live a supernatural life. You also said in Your Word that if I asked You for the Holy Spirit, You would give Him to me. I hereby ask You for the gift of the Holy Spirit. I receive Him now in my life. I am filled with the Holy Spirit. Thank You. Amen.

Now, begin to pray in tongues. The gift is there. You should expect any number of the gifts of the Spirit, but especially the gift of tongues.

Do All Speak in Tongues?

Someone may ask, "Considering the apostle Paul's question *'Do all speak in tongues?'* (1 Corinthians 12:30), how can you say that all Christians should speak in tongues?" In this passage, Paul was talking about public ministry gifts that are manifested in the church. He was not talking about tongues as the initial sign of the baptism in the Spirit, nor was he talking about tongues as a private, devotional prayer language.

You can recognize the truth in this simply by considering the language Paul used concerning speaking in tongues. In this chapter, he called speaking in tongues *"different kinds of tongues"* (1 Corinthians 12:10, 28). *"Different kinds"* implies something other than the "usual kind," which is a language no man understands or interprets. However, speaking in *"different kinds"* of tongues enables the speaker or someone else to recognize the meaning of the tongue, thereby interpreting it.

So, when Paul asked the question, *"Do all speak in tongues?"* he was referring to the public manifestation of tongues that enables a person gifted in interpretation to voice the meaning of the tongue. Not every believer receives this gift of *"different kinds of tongues."*

In 1 Corinthians 14, Paul corrected the misuse of tongues in the church. He told the believers to stop the practice of gathering *"the whole church...together...*[so] *everyone speaks in tongues"* (1 Corinthians 14:23). Notice that *"the whole church"* was gathered and that *"everyone"* was speaking in tongues. This clearly shows that all believers in the Corinthian church were speaking in tongues. Most of them should have allowed those who were gifted in *"different kinds"* of tongues to exercise their gift, while the rest of them simply *"*[kept] *quiet in the church and* [spoke] *to* [themselves] *and God"* (1 Corinthians 14:28) in tongues. Friend, I encourage you to seek the scriptural evidence of the baptism in the Holy Spirit and to settle for nothing less. Tongues will take you to a deeper dimension in your prayer life, enabling you to pray the perfect will of God every time.

Chapter 8

The Prayer of Intercession

I urge, then, first of all, that requests, prayers, intercession and thanksgiving be made for everyone.
—1 Timothy 2:1

Intercession is the act of praying for others. The prayer of intercession usually takes more time than any other prayer. The reason is simple: there is only one of you, and there are billions of other people you could be praying for. You will never develop a great prayer life if your prayers focus only on yourself.

Church prayer meetings are often sparsely attended, which is indicative of the overall selfishness of Christians. Most people, unless they have a personal need, will come up with any excuse to avoid a prayer meeting. But prayer meetings are the foundation of the church. Your church will never mature in a spiritual sense beyond the maturity of the congregation's prayer life. Without corporate prayer, your church may grow in numbers but not in holiness.

Intercession Is Other-Focused

An intercessor needs to be selfless. Most people tend to be selfish, concerning themselves solely with their own lives.

It's like the man who prayed, "Lord, bless me and my wife, and my son and his wife. Bless us four and no more." In intercession, you are praying for *"everyone,"* including people you do not particularly like. Jesus said, *"Love your enemies and pray for those who persecute you"* (Matthew 5:44). Intercession is praying *"for"* people, not against them. You must never pray for judgment to come. Instead, leave judgment up to God (see, for example, Hebrews 10:30) while you pray for His blessings on your enemies.

Paul urged the church at Corinth to intercede *"for kings and all those in authority, that we may live peaceful and quiet lives in all godliness and holiness"* (1 Timothy 2:2). It is obvious that leaders have an especially great need of prayer because their actions and decisions affect many people. In Paul's day, not every ruler was wise and benevolent, much like modern-day politicians, yet Paul urged believers to pray for them, anyway. You cannot pick and choose which leaders "deserve" your prayers; you must pray for all of them.

Praying for others, including political leaders, *"is good, and pleases God our Savior, who wants all men to be saved and to come to a knowledge of the truth"* (1 Timothy 2:3–4). Here is the goal of intercession: the salvation of others. This goal should be more important to you than getting a new job or coming through a surgical operation successfully. Of course, you should pray about those things, too, but the majority of your focus should be on intercessory prayer for others' salvation.

"For there is one God and one mediator between God and men, the man Christ Jesus" (1 Timothy 2:5). Here, Paul contrasted the role of the believer as an intercessor with the role of Christ as mediator. Christ is the ultimate mediator and

intercessor. "*Therefore* [Jesus Christ] *is able to save completely those who come to God through him, because he always lives to intercede for them*" (Hebrews 7:25). While Christ is the only mediator and intercessor, He enjoins us to participate in His intercessory role by praying for others. In this way, intercession is akin to sacrifice. It is our sacrifice for the world. In no way am I suggesting that our prayers for others are on the same level as Christ's sacrifice on the cross, only that they are a *type* of sacrifice. Here is the important point: just as there is no salvation without the cross, so there will be no salvation for others unless we intercede on their behalf in prayer.

The Ultimate Goal of Intercession

I looked for a man among them who would build up the wall and stand before me in the gap on behalf of the land so I would not have to destroy it, but I found none. So I will pour out my wrath on them and consume them with my fiery anger, bringing down on their own heads all they have done, declares the Sovereign LORD.
(Ezekiel 22:30–31)

God looks for someone to "*stand...in the gap on behalf of the land.*" "Standing in the gap" is an apt illustration of the job of an intercessor. There is a gap, after all, between mankind and God—a chasm caused by human sinfulness—which no one may cross without suffering divine wrath. Isaiah echoed the same problem that Ezekiel saw: "*I looked, but there was no one to help, I was appalled that no one gave support; so my own arm worked salvation for me*" (Isaiah 63:5). In the end, there was no one in the world who could stand in the gap for the human race. God alone could do it. And He did, of course, at the cross, which bridged the gap and made it possible for us to cross over into the realm of God's mercy and grace. God, in the person of Jesus Christ, filled the gap of judgment by dying on the cross for our sins. Through Christ's death, the gap has been filled. A bridge has been built. The only thing left is for people to cross over it.

And that's where you come in. You pray for people to cross the bridge of salvation. God uses your prayers to extend the bridge to others. You are not building a *new* bridge but praying for the extension of the *only* bridge that brings people to salvation. This means that only those who have been saved may intercede effectively for other people. While unsaved people may pray for others, they cannot truly intercede.

Delaying Destruction

Sodom was primed for destruction at the hand of God. No one was there to intercede on behalf of the city. When God told Abraham His plans to bring final judgment upon Sodom, Abraham was less than thrilled, and he tried talking God out of His decision. Abraham knew of the city's wicked ways, yet he interceded on behalf of its citizens, pleading that God would show them mercy.

From Abraham's example, we see that a true intercessor never delights in God's judgment on other people. As it says in Proverbs 24:17, *"Do not gloat when your enemy falls; when he stumbles, do not let your heart rejoice."* Desire to see God's mercy, never His judgment, on the lives of others when interceding for them.

This story also illustrates that God will take the initiative by prompting us to pray. It was God who brought up the conversation with Abraham regarding His plans to judge Sodom:

> *When the men got up to leave, they looked down toward Sodom, and Abraham walked along with them to see them on their way. Then the* LORD *said, "Shall I hide from Abraham what I am about to do?"*
> (Genesis 18:16–17)

Often, things are hidden from us, and we are not aware of impending judgment in the lives of others. In these cases, God may reveal to us areas of possible judgment, so that we may pray as intercessors, in hopes of delaying the act of judgment or even canceling it altogether. If you notice that you have someone on your mind, it may be that God is prompting you to pray for that person. Don't ignore divine nudges.

> *The men turned away and went toward Sodom, but Abraham remained standing before the* LORD. *Then Abraham approached him and said: "Will you sweep away the righteous with the wicked?"* (Genesis 18:22–23)

Although all intercession is initiated by God, we must respond by taking action, like Abraham did: *"Abraham approached him."* There is also a "pressing in" that we must do. It isn't all God. Even though God approaches you first, You must be willing to approach God, as well, and press in as you pray.

Abraham knew the difference between the saved and unsaved, and he asked God, *"Will you sweep away the righteous with the wicked?"* The issue was whether his nephew Lot, and others he had led to God, were enough to keep judgment from coming upon the entire city.

> *Then Abraham spoke up again: "Now that I have been so bold as to speak to the Lord, though I am nothing but dust and ashes…."* (Genesis 18:27)

"*I am nothing but dust and ashes.*" In the prayer of faith, you need faith. In the prayer of agreement, you need the co-operation of others. In the prayer in the Spirit, you need the gift of tongues. However, in the prayer of intercession, you need humility. It's the most important character trait of an intercessor. There is no room for pride.

Think about it: you are saved, and you are praying for those who are not yet saved. It may be tempting to think more highly of yourself than the people you are praying for. While it may be true that you are saved, that is only because of God's grace, not because of your works. (See Ephesians 2:8–9.) So, you must maintain a true sense of humility and compassion for those who are not yet saved. A sense of superiority will only hinder your effectiveness in intercession.

Along with humility, Abraham expressed boldness: "*Now that I have been so bold as to speak to the Lord.*" Boldness is a complete confidence in your right to enter into God's presence. Because you have been saved, you have the right to pray and intercede for others. Do not let a sense of failure or guilt over past sins steal your confidence in praying for others.

What happened to Sodom and Gomorrah? Of course, we know that these cities were destroyed. But Abraham's nephew Lot was spared because of Abraham's intercession. This means that even if we don't see everything we hope for, we will see results. You may pray for revival in a city, or for a certain godly man or woman to get elected mayor, only to see dozens of saloons opening all over town or a different man or woman elected mayor. Even so, God can do something good with your prayers. Do not get discouraged if you do not see everything you desire come to fruition. Keep on praying, humbly and boldly!

Delaying Judgment

Israel had dishonored God by distrusting His ability to bring them into the Promised Land. So, God threatened to judge Israel and remove them as a nation. The reason God relented was that Moses interceded for Israel.

> [Moses said,] "Now may the Lord's strength be displayed, just as you have declared: 'The LORD is slow to anger, abounding in love and forgiving sin and rebellion. Yet he does not leave the guilty unpunished; he punishes the children for the sin of the fathers to the third and fourth generation.' In accordance with your great love, forgive the sin of these people, just as you have pardoned them from the time they left Egypt until now." The LORD replied, "I have forgiven them, as you asked."
> (Numbers 14:17–20)

One man made all the difference. How did Moses manage to talk God out of destroying Israel?

Moses appealed to God's immutability.

> [Moses said,] "If you put these people to death all at one time, the nations who have heard this report about you will say, 'The LORD was not able to bring these people into the land he promised them on oath; so he slaughtered them in the desert.'"
> (Numbers 14:15–16)

Moses held God to His Word, reminding Him that He had "promised...on oath" to give them the land and to make them into a great nation. God cannot resist this type of prayer, with its appeal to His faithfulness in upholding His Word. It is the kind of prayer that moves Him.

When I pray for others, I always like to use the Word of God, reminding the Lord of His promises to His children. If you do not know what God has promised, it makes it difficult to pray for others. Begin to study God's promises in Scripture for such blessings as health, financial provision, marriage, children, and deliverance. Search the Bible for what it says regarding those areas and then have the corresponding Scriptures ready when you pray for others. Say something like,

> Father, You have said in Your Word that You will bless our food and water and take sickness away from us. So, I ask You to remove this illness from so-and-so.

When you base your prayers on God's promises, it gives you grounds of assurance as you intercede for others.

Depending on Christ's Sacrifice

Israel became alarmed when they heard that the Philistines wanted to attack them. *"Then Samuel said, 'Assemble all Israel at Mizpah and I will intercede with the LORD for you'"* (1 Samuel 7:5). The answer was intercession. Let's look at the two steps to successful intercession, as illustrated in the example of Samuel.

First, Samuel poured water: *"When they had assembled at Mizpah, they drew water and poured it out before the LORD"* (1 Samuel 7:6). Water represents the Word of God. For instance, you receive *"washing with water through the word"* (Ephesians 5:26).

Next, Samuel made a sacrifice:

> *Then Samuel took a suckling lamb and offered it up as a whole burnt offering to the LORD. He cried out to the*

LORD on Israel's behalf, and the LORD answered him.
(1 Samuel 7:9)

The act of intercession was connected to a sacrifice. In the same way, every prayer of intercession is connected to a sacrifice—the sacrifice of Jesus Christ on Calvary's cross. Samuel's intercessory prayers were answered in Israel's victory over the Philistines because he had connected them to a sacrifice by making a burnt offering. Never leave out the blood of Christ or underestimate its importance in intercession, for *"without the shedding of blood there is no forgiveness"* (Hebrews 9:22).

Delivering Healing

King Jeroboam rejected the Word of God spoken through a man of God. As the king reached out to grab him, his hand shriveled. Now sorry for having rejected God's Word, Jeroboam asked the same man of God,

> *"Intercede with the LORD your God and pray for me that my hand may be restored." So the man of God interceded with the LORD, and the king's hand was restored and became as it was before.*   (1 Kings 13:6)

It is good and proper to pray for the healing of other people. Anyone who has ever been sick knows the feeling of desperation to be well again. We must pray for people to be healed.

The story of King Jeroboam illustrates that when other people ask us to pray, they are granting us a measure of authority in their lives. Even though King Jeroboam was rebellious against God, he had some respect for the man of God and received blessings through him.

An acquaintance of mine had a daughter who was gravely ill. His wife also suffered from mental illness. Yet, even though this man knew that God uses me to bring healing, he refused to ask me to pray for his family. He preferred to argue Scriptures with me rather than use the Word of God to encourage his family.

I asked him, "When are you going to ask me to pray for your family?"

He replied, "God can heal them without you praying. If you want to pray, you can pray for them anytime from your prayer closet."

I wanted him to agree to let me lay hands on his wife and daughter, but he never permitted me to come and pray for them.

Tragedy struck when his wife committed suicide.

Jesus said, *"Anyone who receives a prophet because he is a prophet will receive a prophet's reward, and anyone who receives a righteous man because he is a righteous man will receive a righteous man's reward"* (Matthew 10:41). When you receive the prayers of someone else, you thereby grant that person greater authority over your life than he would have had by merely praying on his own for you, regardless of whether you have granted him permission to do so. That's why it is important to secure the agreement of the people for whom you are praying, whenever possible. While your prayers may still prove effective without the consent of the people for whom you are praying, their power is enhanced significantly when others receive your prayers willingly.

Sometimes, people say to me, "If God gave you power to heal the sick, why don't you just go to the hospital and heal everyone?" This kind of comment indicates an ignorance about the law of responsibility and authority. The more responsible you are, the more authority you have. If someone opens himself to your prayers, then you have more authority in his life, and your prayers are likelier to be answered.

Personal Benefits of Interceding

Job's problems effectively ended when he prayed for his friends.

> *After Job had prayed for his friends, the* LORD *made him prosperous again and gave him twice as much as he had before.* (Job 42:10)

Here is a great secret: God rewards you when you pray for others. I know it seems that you work so hard praying for everyone else, but God will bless you for taking the time to pray for others. If the church really understood this truth, every prayer meeting would be full.

I am convinced that prosperity would come more quickly if we would devote more time to praying for other people. You might be someone who is always seeking prayers from others. If you find that these prayers mostly go unanswered, you may want to consider shifting the focus from yourself to others. Start setting aside time to pray for other people. When you do, God will see to it that you are blessed, as well.

Wrestling in Intercessory Prayer

> *Epaphras, who is one of you and a servant of Christ Jesus, sends greetings. He is always wrestling in prayer for you, that you may stand firm in all the will of God, mature and fully assured.* (Colossians 4:12)

Wrestling was the hardest sport I've ever participated in. Compared to wrestling, baseball, basketball, and even football seemed easy. And I can tell you from experience that praying for others is the hardest type of prayer, because there is lots of wrestling involved. But you can't give up.

The Greek word for "*wrestling*" is *agonizomai*, from which we get the word *agonize*. You will agonize in prayer for others. You will feel their pain when you pray for them. Deep intercession is painful, but it's necessary. This is why successful intercession is never just a short little prayer for someone else. Short, simple prayers are fine, from time to time, but you must be willing to give yourself over to the Holy Spirit and let Him agonize through you. "*The Spirit himself intercedes for us with groans that words cannot express*" (Romans 8:26). Notice the word "*groans.*" Groaning is a sound that someone makes when he is in painful agony.

Personal Prayer "Groanings"

I have learned to let the Lord groan through me. Sometimes, I literally groan in prayer. I don't recommend doing this publicly. On occasion, though, in private moments with God, I have been known to groan.

In high school, two of my classmates were atheists who would always make fun of my faith. I tried witnessing to them, but nothing seemed to work. Then, one day, God led me into a time of deep intercession for them. I groaned loudly and wept uncontrollably for them. This lasted for several minutes.

Two years after high school graduation, I started my church. After several months, one of the guys, Jerry, visited a service. I was so excited—and surprised—to see him. After the service, he told me that he was working for NASA and that he had come to visit his family and wanted to see me.

"Why did you come to my church?" I asked him. "Why did you want to see me?"

He replied, "Tom, I became a Christian. I wanted to come and personally tell you that I gave my life to Christ."

Tears of joy filled my eyes as Jerry told me how he had been converted. I cannot help but wonder if my groaning in intercession had played a small role in bringing him to Christ. I don't know for sure, but I do believe we would see more people come to salvation if we were to yield ourselves more fully to the Holy Spirit, and if we were more apt to groan in pain and wrestle in prayer for those who are lost.

Jesus' Prayer "Groanings"

In Mark 7, there is an account of Jesus healing a mute man. "[Jesus] *looked up to heaven and with a deep sigh said to him, 'Ephphatha!' (which means, 'Be opened!'). At this, the man's ears were opened, his tongue was loosened and he began to speak plainly"* (Mark 7:34–35). Jesus did not offer a quick prayer for this man's healing. Instead, He looked up to heaven and, *"with a deep sigh,"* commanded the man's ears, "Be opened!" The words *"deep sigh"* imply the idea of deep grief and groaning. I believe that Jesus was in deep intercession for the man and that this was why His words had faith and power. I am convinced that our words of faith would have much more power behind them if we would enter into this deep area of intercession.

Jesus experienced something similar at the tomb of Lazarus.

> *When Jesus saw her weeping, and the Jews who had*
> *come along with her also weeping, he was deeply moved*
> *in spirit and troubled. "Where have you laid him?" he*
> *asked. "Come and see, Lord," they replied. Jesus wept.*
>   (John 11:33–35)

Jesus was *"deeply moved in spirit."* There must have been some external indication that Jesus was being moved in His spirit, perhaps by feelings of grief. I think He was agonizing in the Spirit. He probably groaned in the Spirit. Finally, He *"wept."* This was the ultimate expression of intercession. Have you wept for the lost? Are you grieved in your spirit when you see people who are not experiencing the fullness of God's blessings? Let your grief move you to pray deeply in the Spirit.

Chapter 9

The Prayer of Binding and Loosing

I will give you the keys of the kingdom of heaven; whatever you bind on earth will be bound in heaven, and whatever you loose on earth will be loosed in heaven.
—Matthew 16:19

It could be argued that "binding and loosing" is not really prayer but an authority given to us by God. In the prayer of binding and loosing, the words we utter are directed toward Satan. In the Lord's Prayer, we are taught to pray, "*Lead us not into temptation, but deliver us from the evil one*" (Matthew 6:13). The prayer of binding and loosing is the means by which God fulfills this request.

People are often uncomfortable talking directly to the devil. Yet Jesus spoke to him on numerous occasions in the Bible, saying, for example, "*Get behind me, Satan!*" (Matthew 16:23) and "*Away from me, Satan!*" (Matthew 4:10).

"*Whatever you bind on earth will be bound in heaven, and whatever you loose on earth will be loosed in heaven.*" What does this passage really mean? Jesus was saying that heaven will bind whatever you bind and will loose whatever you loose. The Greek word for "*bind*" means "to fasten with chains," "to forbid," and the word for *"loose"* means "to release," "to allow." In other words, heaven will chain up whatever you chain up and release whatever you release. Heaven also will forbid whatever you forbid and allow whatever you allow.

When tragedy strikes, people often question God, wanting to know why He allowed it to happen. The answer is that God has given us—the church—the power to allow or disallow whatever is of the devil. A lot of things that happen are caused by the devil. We can't blame God for what the devil does. God is not responsible for stopping the devil. We are! The devil is already defeated, but it's our responsibility to bind him in chains.

The Boundaries of Binding

Some theologians limit the usage of binding and loosing to church authority. They confine the concept of binding to the excommunication of people and deny its application to the schemes of Satan. Undoubtedly, this is part of what the word *bind* means; however, the New Testament meaning includes the authority to bind the devil. In other words, whatever the devil causes—be it sickness, demon possession, or some other evil—we have the authority to stop.

Earlier in Matthew's gospel, Jesus said this about binding Satan:

> Or else how can one enter into a strong man's house, and spoil his goods, except he first bind the strong man? and then he will spoil his house.   (Matthew 12:29 KJV)

The *"strong man"* is Satan. He is mentioned in a preceding verse: *"If Satan drives out Satan, he is divided against himself"* (Matthew 12:26).

So, Jesus describes Himself as the One who *"binds"* the strong man. The Greek word translated as *"binds"* is *deo*, and it is found in both Matthew 16:19 and Matthew 12:29. In the first passage, it refers to keys that bind; in the latter, it describes the actions the Lord takes against the strong man. The word *deo* is also used in connection with the devil making people sick. After Jesus had healed a woman from curvature of the spine, He said, *"Then should not this woman, a daughter of Abraham, whom Satan has kept **bound** for eighteen long years, be set free on the Sabbath day from what bound her?"* (Luke 13:16). Jesus described this sick woman as having been *"bound"* by Satan.

In Revelation 20, the same Greek word is used in conjunction with Satan being bound for a thousand years.

> *And I saw an angel coming down out of heaven, having the key to the Abyss and holding in his hand a great chain. He seized the dragon, that ancient serpent, who is the devil, or Satan, and **bound** him for a thousand years.* (Revelation 20:1–2)

The angel *"bound"* Satan with a chain and locked him in the Abyss with a key. It's clear, then, that the authority Christ gave us to bind can be applied to the devil.

Clues in the Keys

Let's go back to the passage in Matthew 16 that talks about the power to bind and loose. Some people point out that Jesus was speaking to Peter about the keys of the kingdom, and, as a result, they assume that Peter was the sole possessor of the keys of the kingdom. While it is true that Peter was the first one to receive the keys from Jesus, He later granted the keys to the rest of His disciples, as well, and said to them, *"I tell you* [the Twelve] *the truth, whatever you bind on earth will be bound in heaven, and whatever you loose on earth will be loosed in heaven"* (Matthew 18:18). This is the same statement that He made to Peter in Matthew 16:19. Thus, Peter was not the sole possessor of the keys to the kingdom. The other disciples received them, as well.

Most people completely misunderstand what the keys of the kingdom can do. Those who claim apostolic succession think that Jesus was giving Peter the right to either admit people into heaven or bar them access. But this is not what the Scripture teaches.

The Keys Are for Earth

Instead of jumping to conclusions concerning the power of the keys of the kingdom, we should allow Jesus to tell us what the keys can do. Let's look once again at the words Jesus spoke to Peter: *"I will give you the keys of the kingdom of heaven; whatever you bind on earth will be bound in heaven"* (Matthew 16:19). You can't use these keys to bind things in heaven; they may be used only to bind things *"on earth."* True, heaven will back up whatever you bind here, but you may directly bind only what is here on earth. We can conclude, then, that these keys have nothing to do with opening the gates of heaven to certain people and keeping them closed to others.

The Keys Give Dominion

Keys represent ownership, which translates to authority and power. When I purchased my house, I was given the keys. This meant that I now had the legal right and power to move into my home. When Jesus said, *"I will give you the keys,"* He meant, in effect, "I will give you authority and power to allow or disallow whatever happens on earth." Jesus used the term *"kingdom of heaven"* to refer to God's sovereign rule over the world. Many people mistakenly assume that this term refers to heaven itself—the spiritual realm we enter into after physical death. Yet this is not the same as the *"kingdom of heaven."*

Jesus often used parables to describe the kingdom of heaven, and none of His parables suggested that this kingdom was the place where believers go after death. The kingdom of heaven is simply the everlasting realm of God's power and authority. *"The kingdom of God is not a matter of talk but of power"* (1 Corinthians 4:20). God's kingdom *is* His power. This means that Jesus was giving us God's heavenly authority and power to bring about God's will on earth.

The Keys Are Plural

I was reading the Scripture about the keys of the kingdom when the Lord spoke to me and asked, *Did you notice that the word "keys" is plural?*

I answered, "No, Lord, I've never noticed that before!"

The Lord continued, *The trouble with My people is that they try to bind and loose with only one key. I gave them more than one key. They should use all the keys that I gave them.*

I asked, "Lord, how many keys did You give us?"

He answered by reminding me of Acts 4:29–31, which I soon realized identifies each of the three keys of the kingdom:

[Peter and John prayed,] *"Now, Lord, consider their threats and enable your servants to speak **your word** with great boldness. Stretch out your hand to heal and perform miraculous signs and wonders through the* *name of your holy servant Jesus." After they prayed, the place where they were meeting was shaken. And they were all filled with the **Holy Spirit** and spoke the word of God boldly.*

Joy filled my heart as I recognized these three keys: the Word of God, the name of Jesus, and the Holy Spirit. You need all three keys to exercise dominion over the devil. You cannot employ just one key and think that everything is going to be all right. You need all three keys. As I meditated on this revelation, the Lord began to make these things clear to me. I realized that the keys represent the three branches of God's government.

For to us a child is born, to us a son is given, and the government will be on his shoulders....Of the increase of his government and peace there will be no end. He will reign on David's throne and over his kingdom, establishing and upholding it with justice and righteousness from that time on and forever. (Isaiah 9:6–7)

Notice that Jesus upholds *"his government."* Don't misread this and think that He upholds human governments. Jesus has His own government, His own kingdom. The keys of the kingdom are the branches of His government. It is through these keys that He rules.

Three Branches of God's Government

Most earthly governments have three branches: legislative, judicial, and executive. In the United States, the legislative branch is the Congress. It makes the laws. The judicial branch is our court system, stretching all the way up to the Supreme Court. It interprets the authority of the laws. Then, there is the executive branch, comprising one man: the president. His job is to enforce the authority of the laws.

With those three branches in mind, you can see the parallels in God's kingdom government: the Word of God is the legislative branch, the name of Jesus is the judicial branch, and the Holy Spirit is the executive branch.

Legislative Branch: The Word of God

The Word of God is the legislative branch in the government of God's kingdom. As such, it decides what you may bind and loose. In Jesus' day, the terms *bind* and *loose* had a legal connotation. To "bind" something was to declare it unlawful; to "loose" something was to sanction it, to declare it lawful. The Word of God tells us what is lawful and unlawful.

The first thing you need to know in order to exercise dominion over the devil is the law, just as a police officer must be familiar with the law in order to enforce it. How can he uphold the law if he does not know what it says? He can't. And the same is true of you. How can you bind Satan if you don't know the law, which is the Word of God? You won't know what is unlawful for Satan if you don't know what it says in the Word of God.

Many people try to exercise dominion over the devil when he brings sickness, poverty, temptation, and other evils. However, unless they are familiar with the Word of God and are standing on what it says, these people will be defeated. When they face sickness, for example, they may say, "Devil, get out of my life, and take your sickness with you!"

Yet the devil responds, "Why should I leave? I don't have to obey you!"

At this point, many sincere Christians don't know any Scriptures to use against the devil. They don't know what the Word of God says about sickness and divine health.

When Jesus was tempted, He simply said, *"It is written..."* and supplied the devil with a scriptural retort. (See Matthew 4:4, 7, 10; Luke 4:4, 8, 10.) Can you say to the devil, "It is written..."? If not, then you definitely have a problem.

You see, the devil is not afraid of you, personally. He is afraid of God. *"You believe that there is one God. Good! Even the demons believe that—and shudder"* (James 2:19). The devil and his demons are afraid of God. If you can't tell them what God has said, then they will continue to hang around you and tempt you, because they are not afraid of you.

Several years ago, our church held its services in a building that housed another tenant. In an act of spite, the other tenant shut off the water. Unfortunately, access to the water line was located on his side of the building.

We called the police, and they sent an officer over. After we had explained the situation to him, he went to the other tenant and asked him if he had turned off the water.

"Yes," he admitted.

"Would you please turn it back on?" the officer asked.

"No."

The officer was shocked but could do nothing. He came back and told me, "Pastor, I have no jurisdiction over the water utilities. The authority over the water belongs to the water company."

I had called the wrong person. The local police could not exercise jurisdiction in the area of utilities. Even though the police officer was armed with a gun, a club, some mace, and a pair of handcuffs, he could not exercise these instruments of power in an area where he had no authority, according to the law.

The only authority that is permitted jurisdiction over the devil is the Word of God. It is the only authority he will listen to. No other word will make the devil obey. Only God's Word can put a stop to Satan's schemes and drive him out.

Judicial Branch: Jesus Christ

The judicial branch of God's kingdom has the authority to make decisions based on the law. This branch is found in the person of Jesus Christ, whom God established as the ultimate Judge: *"For [God] has set a day when he will judge the world with justice by the man he has appointed. He has given proof of this to all men by raising him from the dead"* (Acts 17:31).

The United States Supreme Court is made up of judges who interpret the law. Likewise, Jesus Christ is the interpreter of God's Word and the final authority on what it says. I'm surprised to see so many believers departing from Jesus' utterances of Scripture in favor of drawing their own conclusions. For example, Jesus says, *"In solemn truth I tell you, anyone believing in me shall do the same miracles I have done, and even greater ones, because I am going to be with the Father"* (John 14:12 TLB). Despite the clear promise of Christ, many churches deny that miracles are to be exercised by today's believer. I've heard preachers say, "I believe God can heal, but I don't believe that faith healers can."

What they mean by "faith healers" are those who lay hands on the sick, like Jesus did in Bible times. If a faith healer is someone who believes that God can heal *through* him, then we all ought to be faith healers.

Those who doubt present-day miracles often interpret Scriptures that depict believers possessing miraculous powers in light of their denominational traditions. Instead, they should interpret those Scriptures in light of Christ's authority. He clearly established the Word of God as teaching that all believers may possess God's supernatural power to work miracles.

In the end, you can read, memorize, and preach all the Scriptures you want, but if you reject the teachings of Jesus Christ and disregard His interpretations of Scripture, you have lost a crucial key to binding the work of the devil. You will have made the mistake of the theologians in Jesus' day, to whom Jesus said, *"Woe to you experts in the law, because you have taken away the key to knowledge. You yourselves have not entered, and you have hindered those who were entering"* (Luke 11:52). This situation is still true today. Many sincere believers desire to enter into all the fullness of the gospel— tongues, healing, faith, gifts of the Spirit, spiritual warfare— and yet tradition-bound churches hinder these hungry disciples from pursuing the Spirit-filled life.

Through the name of Jesus, we have all authority to drive out demons and work miracles. Jesus said,

> Go into all the world and preach the good news to all creation. Whoever believes and is baptized will be saved, but whoever does not believe will be condemned. And these signs will accompany those who believe: In my name they will drive out demons; they will speak in new tongues; they will pick up snakes with their hands; and when they drink deadly poison, it will not hurt them at

*all; they will place their hands on sick people, and they
will get well.* (Mark 16:15–18)

How were believers to do these miracles? Jesus made the
answer clear: *"In my name."* We do them in Jesus' name. You
can speak the Word of God and see some results, but you will
see far better results when you speak the Word in the name
of Jesus. Demons listen to the name of Jesus.

Do you abide by the speed limit and other traffic laws? You
might qualify your answer by saying, "Yes, if I see that there's
a police cruiser nearby." It's amazing how slowly most people
drive when there's a police car parked on the side of the road.
That police car represents authority, and authority—especially
when it's present—usually compels people to obey the law.

Drivers roar past speed limit signs all the time, refusing
to abide by the posted limit. Demons behave in much the
same way. You can quote Scripture at them, but they will
ignore you—until you show them the authority you have in
the name of Jesus. When you say, "In the name of Jesus, the
Word of God says such and such," demons listen and obey.
They are just like speeding drivers who suddenly notice a police car parked nearby.

Do you understand the authority you have in the name of
Jesus? The name of Jesus is your badge of authority. A police
officer can stand at an intersection and direct traffic. He lifts
his hand and blows his whistle, and the traffic stops. When
you confidently show your badge of authority to the devil, he
obeys. Your badge is the name of Jesus.

The disciples recognized their authority in Christ. They
said to Jesus, *"Lord, even the demons submit to us in your name"*
(Luke 10:17). In essence, they were saying, "The demons

know that You are the Supreme Court Justice of the kingdom. They obey us when we use Your authority!"

Few people understand what it means to use Jesus' name. His name is not a code word or a magic incantation. The seven sons of Sceva tried to use Jesus' name in this way, and, as a result, they were beaten by a demon-possessed man. (See Acts 19:13–16.)

A name is only as good as the person who bears it. If I handed you a check for a million dollars, would you be excited? Maybe so. But what if I told you that I don't have a million dollars in the bank? My signature, and the million-dollar check, wouldn't mean anything. To understand the value and power in the name of Jesus, you have to understand the wealth and authority of Jesus. You must know what is invested in the name of Jesus. He is worthy, incomparable, and immeasurable, with riches incalculable.

Executive Branch: The Holy Spirit

We now come to the executive branch of God's governmental kingdom—the Holy Spirit. Laws and the authority to interpret them are important, but they mean little if there is no power to enforce them. In the 1960s, the U.S. Supreme Court used its authority to outlaw racial segregation. Nevertheless, many racists refused to allow minorities into their schools, businesses, and organizations. Who came to the aid of the minorities? Not the Supreme Court justices but the president. He sent in the National Guard to ensure the legal rights of minorities.

It is not the job of Christ to enforce the Word of God over the devil—that task falls to the Holy Spirit. Christ Himself said, *"I drive out demons by the Spirit of God"* (Matthew 12:28) and *"By myself I can do nothing"* (John 5:30). Jesus declared that His miracles were done by the power of God's Holy Spirit, not by His own power. In fact, Jesus never performed a miracle until He was filled with the Holy Spirit who empowered Him.

The Holy Spirit is the One with the *power*. Christ is the One with the *authority*. The name of Jesus gives you authority, and the Holy Spirit gives you power to wield that authority. You must drive out demons by the authority of the name of Jesus and through the power of the Holy Spirit.

After Jesus had granted His disciples authority to drive out demons, He instructed them, *"Do not leave Jerusalem, but wait for the gift my Father promised....But you will receive power when the Holy Spirit comes on you"* (Acts 1:4, 8). Jesus did not say that they would receive *authority* but ***"power** when the Holy Spirit"* came on them. The Bible always associates power with the Holy Spirit. He is the One with the power of God.

Just as the disciples needed the power of the Holy Spirit in their lives, we, too, need that same power. We must receive the Spirit in the same way they did. No other way will do. You will never win your battle against the devil without the baptism in the Holy Spirit.

The same was true of Jesus—He needed the Holy Spirit to make Him successful in battling Satan.

> *When all the people were being baptized, Jesus was baptized too. And as he was praying, heaven was opened and the Holy Spirit descended on him in bodily form like a dove....Jesus, full of the Holy Spirit, returned from the Jordan and was led by the Spirit in the desert, where for forty days he was tempted by the devil.*
>
> (Luke 3:21–22; 4:1–2)

Jesus was as much the Son of God before He was baptized and filled with the Spirit as He was afterward. You were as much a child of God before you were baptized and filled with the Spirit as you are now. And, like Jesus, you are not prepared to confront the devil until you are filled with the Spirit. If Christ needed the Holy Spirit to confront Satan, then surely you need the Holy Spirit to defy him, as well.

Never Stop Being Filled

Many believers who would identify themselves as charismatic or Pentecostal stop with the baptism in the Holy Spirit, thinking that they have all there is to have. This would be true if they were to remain filled with the Holy Spirit. Unfortunately, as D. L. Moody once suggested, the reason we need to keep being filled with the Spirit is because our vessels leak.

The apostle Paul admonished the Christians at Ephesus to *"be filled with the Spirit"* (Ephesians 5:18). As a Pentecostal, I was taught that when I had received the Holy Spirit, I had received Him permanently. While it is true that I was filled with the Spirit and spoke in tongues, the Bible makes it clear that one must maintain the Spirit-filled life.

Just because you once spoke in tongues does not mean that you are forever filled with the Spirit. The same book of Acts that had convinced me of my need to be filled with the Spirit also taught me that I needed to *stay* filled with the Spirit. In Acts 4:31, it says, *"And they were all filled with the Holy Spirit and spoke the word of God boldly."* Who were *"they"* that were filled with the Spirit? The apostles and the rest of the disciples. They had already been filled with the Spirit on the day of Pentecost, so this was *another* infilling, which suggests that they needed to be filled with the Holy Spirit multiple times.

There is a refilling of the Spirit that many Pentecostals know nothing about. The reason you need to be refilled is that you become drained by the trials of life. Every time you encounter a trial, the power of God is released to help you overcome it. As a result, your level of "fullness" diminishes. To restore yourself to your previous level, you need to refill your spiritual life through daily reading of the Word and prayer, as well as through periodic fasting.

The Importance of "Refilling"

A great example of this truth in action is the story of Paul on the island of Malta, where he ended up after a shipwreck. As the ship was sailing past the island, Paul and the others on board were in mortal danger of losing their lives in the terrible storm that was tossing the ship to and fro. But Paul maintained faith that they would be safe, and they were. The ship was destroyed, though, forcing its occupants to swim for shore.

But Paul's trials were not yet over. He built a fire for warmth, and when he reached for some brushwood to rekindle the flame, he was bitten by a poisonous viper. Paul apparently remembered Jesus' assurance that those who believed could take up serpents and drink poison without suffering harm. So, Paul stood on God's Word, and he suffered no ill effects. This miracle caused others to treat Paul hospitably, and he was even welcomed into the home of the chief official—where yet another miracle would occur.

"[The official's] *father was sick in bed, suffering from fever and dysentery. Paul went in to see him and, after prayer, placed his hands on him and healed him*" (Acts 28:8). Once, when I was reading this account, I noticed something unusual: Paul did not place his hands on the man until *after* he had prayed. Then, it hit me! Paul was so spiritually drained in the wake of the shipwreck and the snake bite that he was not quite ready to lay hands on this man. He needed to pray first. After he had prayed, he was ready to heal the man. Through prayer, Paul *refilled* his store of spiritual power and was subsequently able to exercise God's power to heal the man.

I wonder how many of us are wise enough to spend time in prayer before we attempt to manifest a miracle. Prayer refills our lives with the power of God so that we have the power necessary to overcome Satan's works.

The Importance of Praying and Fasting

You may recall the incident when the disciples tried in vain to drive out an evil spirit. (See, for example, Matthew 17:14–18.) After Jesus successfully drove it out, the disciples asked Him, "*Why couldn't we drive it out?*" (Matthew 17:19). The word *"couldn't"* implies a lack of ability, not a lack of authority. The disciples had tried to use the authority of the name of Jesus, but the name was not sufficient in this case. Jesus affirmed this fact when He said that *"this kind* [of demon] *does not go out except by prayer and fasting"* (Matthew 7:21 NKJV). Jesus was explaining that it is sometimes necessary to supplement His name with prayer and fasting. Instead of devoting themselves to prayer and fasting, these disciples had wasted time arguing with the skeptics over religion. (See Mark 9:14.) Jesus, on the other hand, had evidently spent time praying and fasting on the Mount of Transfiguration. He was prepared with power to cast out the demon.

There are certain demons that will not submit to the name of Jesus. I know that sounds almost blasphemous, but it's true. Some spirits are so rebellious that the only thing strong enough to drive them out of people is pure Holy Spirit power, and this kind of power comes through prayer and fasting.

A young couple in our church learned firsthand the power in fasting. The Guillens had a beautiful daughter who had been born with a large lump on the side of her neck—a massive growth that detracted from her pretty features. The Guillens prayed diligently for her healing, yet nothing changed in their daughter's appearance.

Then, one day, I received a call from them. They said, "Pastor, our little girl is healed! The growth is gone!" The next day, they shared their wonderful testimony with our church. With my own eyes, I can verify this healing. There she was— perfectly healed, with no visible trace of where the growth had been!

The thing that impressed me most was not the healing but how it came about. This is the Guillens' testimony:

> The Lord laid upon our hearts the need to fast for our daughter. We didn't know much about fasting, but we did it anyway. The moment we began to fast, our daughter began to complain that her neck was hurting. Soon, she was screaming in pain. The soft growth turned hard. We were concerned, but we knew that God had called us to fast for our daughter, and we knew she would be healed. One morning, we noticed that the growth was a little smaller. The next day, it shrank even more. Finally, the growth disappeared altogether.

I am convinced that the Guillens' fasting brought about their daughter's healing. Fasting increased the power of God in their lives so that they were able to drive out the growth from their daughter.

Blessed with Dominion

I'm sure you have noticed by now that the three keys represent the three persons of the Trinity: the Word of God the *Father*; the name of *Jesus*, His Son; and the power of the *Holy Spirit*. By having a relationship with the fullness of the Godhead, you receive the three keys of the kingdom.

Just before the creation of man, God spoke on behalf of the Trinity in the first-person plural, saying, *"Let **us** make man in **our** image"* (Genesis 1:26). The first words the Trinity spoke to mankind were a blessing: *"God blessed them and said to them, 'Be fruitful and increase in number; fill the earth and subdue it"* (Genesis 1:28).

The last words Jesus spoke to humanity before He ascended to heaven were also a blessing: *"When [Jesus] had led them out to the vicinity of Bethany, he lifted up his hands and blessed them"* (Luke 24:50).

This blessing came on the tails of Jesus' Great Commission to His disciples:

> Go into all the world and preach the good news to all creation. Whoever believes and is baptized will be saved, but whoever does not believe will be condemned. And these signs will accompany those who believe: In my name they will drive out demons; they will speak in new tongues; they will pick up snakes with their hands; and when they drink deadly poison, it will not hurt them at

all; they will place their hands on sick people, and they
will get well. (Mark 16:15–18)

Do you see the connection between the first "great commission" in Genesis and the last Great Commission in the Gospels? The Trinity blessed God's followers with *dominion*. Dominion means having both the authority and power to govern and control. Through the power of the Godhead—the three keys of God's government—you can be effective in waging war against the devil and count on securing a victory.

Part II

Principles of Answered Prayer

Chapter 10

A Universal Principle of Prayer

Pray in the Spirit on all occasions
with all kinds of prayers and requests.
—Ephesians 6:18

I was a senior in high school when I first heard Rev. Kenneth E. Hagin teach on different types of prayer. I listened to his sermon on cassette tape in the back room of my grandparents' house, which my grandfather had built from adobe brick in the early 1900s. It was a simple structure without any halls; just a rectangle with five rooms: a living room, a kitchen, and two bedrooms, with a bathroom adjoining them. Later, as the family grew, my grandfather added two more rooms, off of the back of the house. One room was his bedroom, and the other room was a space we called "the back room." There was neither central heating nor air-conditioning in that house. The only warmth came from a portable heater in the living room. On a cold day, to stay warm, you nestled near the heater, warming yourself like a camper rubbing his hands together over a campfire.

Looking back, I see that the house had a certain charm to it. At the time, however, I just viewed it as "old." The back room was especially uncomfortable in cold weather. Although it was a bit chilly that day, Rev. Hagin's message warmed me. The revelation I received that morning changed my life forever.

The Prayer Must Depend on the Situation

Speaking on Ephesians 6:18, Hagin explained that there are different *"kinds of prayers,"* just as there are different kinds of sports. You wouldn't play football according to the rules of baseball. In the same way, each type of prayer has its own "rules" and methods that make it appropriate for specific situations. Hagin referenced the prayer that Jesus prayed in the garden of Gethsemane when He said, *"Yet not my will, but yours be done"* (Luke 22:42). Hagin said that many Christians tack on the phrase "if it is Your will" when they pray for health, failing to realize that the prayer for health should not be governed by the prayer that Jesus prayed in the garden. Hagin explained that, in the garden, Jesus was not praying to change things; He was praying to dedicate Himself to the will of God—a prayer of submission. Whenever He prayed for healing, He never spoke of God's will. He knew that healing was always God's will. There was never a question about it.

Yet believers have been questioning God's will regarding healing for millennia. For example, a leper asked Jesus to heal him, saying, *"Lord, if you are willing, you can make me clean"* (Matthew 8:2). Notice that the leper used the phrase *"if you are willing."* This man was unsure whether it was God's will to heal him. I am glad that this man's doubts were recorded, because most of us can identify with those feelings. Most of us, at one time or another, have doubted God's will to heal. Jesus, however, removed all doubt concerning God's willingness to heal: *"Jesus reached out his hand and touched the man. 'I am willing,' he said. 'Be clean!' Immediately he was cured of his leprosy"*

(Matthew 8:3). *The New Testament in Modern English*, by J. B. Phillips, is even more emphatic in its translation of Jesus' response: *"Of course I want to."* Jesus seemed almost offended that the leper would doubt His willingness to heal.

As I combed through the Scriptures, looking for every instance in which Jesus healed someone, I noticed that He always healed when asked to do so, and He usually attributed people's healing to their own faith.

Remember that *"faith is being sure of what we hope for and certain of what we do not see"* (Hebrews 11:1). Faith is being certain that something will happen. How can someone be *"sure"* if he is *unsure* of God's will? At first, the leper was unsure, but, when he heard Jesus assure him of His willingness to heal him, I believe his doubt vanished and was immediately replaced by faith.

Rev. Hagin explained that God's will is always for His children to be healed. To be unsure of God's will in this matter is really to wear a "badge of doubt." And a person who doubts *"should not think he will receive anything from the Lord"* (James 1:7).

When I heard this, I was convicted. Like many, I was accustomed to using the faith-destroying phrase, "If it is Your will, please heal so-and-so." I never realized that I was taking the rules that governed the prayer of submission and misapplying them to the prayer of faith.

Developing Effectiveness with Different Kinds of Prayer

I have come to realize that it is possible to be gifted at praying a particular kind of prayer but ineffective at praying another type of prayer, in the same way that someone can excel at one sport but fall short in another. Michael Jordan was possibly the greatest basketball player ever, yet his professional baseball stint proved to be a failure. Like Michael and his basketball skills, there are believers who are skilled at praying prayers of submission but mediocre when it comes to prayers of faith. Other believers may be good at praying the prayer of intercession but unable to pray in the Spirit. Some believers are great at praying prayers of petition but grow shy when it comes to prayers of binding and loosing.

Practice, Practice, Practice

When I was young, I was fairly good at baseball—hitting, in particular. I had quick reflexes and excellent hand-eye coordination. Because of my skills, I was usually the lead-off batter in the lineup. When I took up golfing, I thought it would be a "piece of cake." After all, I could hit a fast-moving baseball without a problem; surely, I could hit a golf ball sitting still on a tee. At first, however, I had a hard time hitting that stationary little ball. And, on the rare occasion I managed to hit it off of the tee, it sliced to the right or hooked to the left. While I was good at baseball, I needed a lot of practice to become proficient at golf. In time, I did get a little better.

Practice makes perfect in prayer, as well. You may be quite gifted at praying prayers of faith, but perhaps you need some practice with prayers of submission. My goal is to help you to increase your effectiveness with each of the different kinds of prayers and to teach you the rules and principles that govern them all.

Don't Presume to Be an Expert

Let me caution you not to get cocky when you think you have learned something about prayer. You may not have gotten it exactly right. This reminds me of another true golf story.

My golf instructor, Mark, took my wife, Sonia, and me to the driving range, where we practiced driving golf balls. I so badly wanted to learn how to putt, but Mark told me that unless we could drive the ball, putting would not be important. For several weeks, we practiced with our drivers. Finally, Mark allowed us to putt.

"When are we going to go to the golf course to play?" I asked Mark.

"Soon."

I was beginning to get impatient and felt that Mark was slowing our progress, so I called him and asked, "I know we are not ready to do all eighteen holes, but is there a shorter game?"

"Well, there is the 'back nine'; you could play only half of the holes."

"Okay, Mark," I said. "I feel we're ready. I'm going to take Sonia to the golf course to play the back nine."

"If you think you're ready, have fun," he said, "and let me know how you did."

At the golf course, Sonia and I rented a cart, pulled out the map, and tried to find where we needed to be.

Looking over my shoulder, Sonia asked, "Honey, where do we begin?"

"Hmm. If we want to play the back nine, I suppose we have to start at the end." I pointed to the map. "Uh, here is the eighteenth hole. I guess we tee off there." Without questioning my "expertise," Sonia got in the cart, and we drove to the tee box of the eighteenth hole.

Now, if you are a golfer, I know you are cringing at this. You're thinking, *Are you kidding? That's not how you play the back nine!*

Well, that's how we played it. And it took a long time!

Whenever we finally finished playing one hole, we would pull out the map and locate the tee box of the previous hole. Eighteen...seventeen...sixteen...fifteen...fourteen...thirteen...you get the idea.

Finally, growing tired, I spoke up. "Sonia, this is taking us longer than I expected. It seems to me that it would be much faster to play the next hole rather than go backward. I don't know why they invented the back nine; it takes longer to play this way than to play all eighteen holes." Nevertheless, we weaved our cart past many a confused-looking golfer, looking for the tee for the twelfth hole.

Spotting a golfer alone in his cart, we pulled over and asked, "Where is the twelfth hole?"

He looked puzzled. "Where are you coming from?"

"Oh, we just finished the thirteenth. Now, we are looking for the twelfth."

His eyebrows arched in confusion. "Why would you finish the thirteenth hole and then go backward?"

"Oh, that's easy. We're playing the back nine."

At that point, the man looked around, as if trying to spot a hidden camera. He must have figured we were part of an elaborate joke. Then, realizing it was no gag, the man looked at us again, grinned a little, and said, in the gentlest of tones, "You don't play the back nine that way."

"We don't?"

"No. You start at the tenth hole and play forward to the eighteenth hole."

Uh-oh!

Sonia gave me one of the ugliest looks I have ever gotten from her. She was humiliated because of her "expert" husband and his decision to play the back nine—backward! Needless to say, we were too embarrassed to finish the course.

This story is meant to illustrate what happens when we presume to know how to do something but really don't. Often, we think we know how to pray in a certain situation when, in reality, we still need to learn. I don't want you to embarrass yourself by praying "backward."

Three Reasons to Pray

There are three reasons to pray: (1) to change *circumstances*; (2) to change *other people*; and (3) to change *yourself.* In the end, the purpose of all prayer is to bring about change. In fact, prayer has failed if no change whatsoever takes place. However, you must know that certain types of prayer work better than others in certain instances. You are bound to experience frustration if you pray the type of prayer that changes circumstances when your desire is really for other people to change.

Below is a simple diagram of the three reasons to pray, along with the corresponding types of prayer that work best in each category. Keep in mind that some types of prayer can work well in multiple categories, and that this chart should not be treated as a formula. There are even some prayers that are effective in multiple categories—for example, praying in the Spirit, which is also called "praying in tongues." This type of prayer is effective when you are praying for others, especially when you are unsure of God's perfect will for them. Meanwhile, according to the apostle Paul, by praying in the Spirit, you yourself are edified: *"He who speaks in a tongue edifies himself"* (1 Corinthians 14:4). Praying in tongues has a twofold purpose of benefitting others and yourself.

Prayers to Change Circumstances	Prayers to Change Other People	Prayers to Change Yourself
Prayer in the Spirit (Ephesians 6:18)	Prayer in the Spirit (Ephesians 6:18)	The Prayer of Submission (Matthew 26:39)
The Prayer of Petition (Philippians 4:6)	The Prayer of Intercession (1 Timothy 2:1)	The Prayer of Release (1 Peter 5:7)
The Prayer of Faith (Mark 11:24)	The Prayer of Agreement (Matthew 18:19)	The Prayer of Praise (Acts 13:2)
The Prayer of Agreement (Matthew 18:19)	The Prayer of Binding and Loosing (Matthew 18:18)	The Prayer of Agreement (Matthew 18:19)
The Prayer of Binding and Loosing (Matthew 18:18)		The Prayer of Binding and Loosing (Matthew 18:18)

Chapter 11

Why Some Prayers Go Unanswered

Prayers are meant to be answered. There really is no point in praying if God isn't going to answer us. The Bible gives a record of many prayers, most of which were answered. There were only a few exceptions. In the cases of prayers not being answered, it was often the people who prayed who were at fault. God is never to blame for unanswered prayer. Not only does the Bible record many instances of answered prayers, but the same Scriptures also promise that God is faithful to answer our prayers today. Jesus said, *"For everyone who asks receives; he who seeks finds; and to him who knocks, the door will be opened"* (Matthew 7:8; Luke 11:10). Yet we have to admit that not everyone who has asked has also received. Perhaps you can recall some of your own prayers that went unanswered—for example, a prayer for a sick relative who subsequently died, a prayer for the restoration of a marriage that later ended in divorce, or a prayer for wisdom concerning a situation in which your decision turned out to be bad.

The point that Jesus was making was that every *right* prayer has the potential to be answered. God wants everyone who prays to get a response. Yet many people are plagued with wondering why their prayers come up empty.

Six Possible Explanations for Unanswered Prayer

There are six basic reasons that some prayers go unanswered:

1. God May Not Want to Answer the Prayer

It's that's simple. It's your job to pray, but it is God's job to answer. If a prayer goes unanswered, it could simply be that God has a reason for not answering it. There is always a reason why it is not His will to answer.

2. Inappropriate Prayer for a Particular Situation

It is possible that you prayed a prayer that was not appropriate for the need. For example, if you request something of the government using the wrong form, don't be surprised if your request goes unfulfilled. You can't use a tax form to request a court hearing. You can't use a gun registration to get a driver's license. You have to use the appropriate form before the government will consider your petition, let alone grant it. In the same way, you have to use the right prayer for the situation.

3. Praying the Wrong Words

Perhaps you said the wrong words, even though your request was legitimate. You must use the proper words with God if your prayers are going to be taken seriously. Leaving something out could cause your prayers to return unfulfilled, in the same way that leaving the recipient's address off of an envelope you're trying to mail could cause the postal service to send the letter back to you, marked "Return to Sender." Even if you used the correct postage, you must address the envelope properly if you expect it to reach its destination.

4. Impure Motives of the Heart

Your heart may not have had pure motives, even though you used the right words for the right request. Unlike the courts or the post office, whose primary concern is that you have filled out the proper forms in the correct manner, God knows the motives of your heart when you come into His presence to present your requests.

5. Conditions for Answered Prayer Unmet

You may not have met a condition that God has set in order for your prayer to be answered. God is not a bellboy who hearkens to your every request. He is the God of the universe, the Judge of heaven and earth. He is over you. So, if He requires something of you before He blesses you, there is no reason to keep pleading with Him unless you have met His conditions. Often, we are the ones hindering our prayers from being answered.

6. Not Belonging to God's Family

You should not expect your prayers to be answered if you do not belong to God's family. The United States government is not obligated to meet the needs of nonresidents. The same is true with God. God requires that we become His children before He will commit to acting as our Father and meeting our needs. Although God is good to everyone, He is especially good to those who are His own.

There is no need to remain unsure of what it takes to receive answers to prayers. Let's examine next some of the most common mistakes that people make when approaching God in prayer. Then, in part III, we will look at concrete steps believers can take in order to receive answers to their prayers.

Chapter 12

Common Mistakes
Praying People Make

Mistake #1: Confusing the Prayer of Submission
with the Prayer of Faith

In chapter 10, I talked about how Rev. Hagin explained the error in applying the rules of the prayer of submission to the prayer of faith. Let's look once more at these two types of prayer to be sure we understand how they differ.

Jesus Prays a Prayer of Submission

Knowing that the cross was set before Him, Jesus prayed in the garden of Gethsemane for God to take away the "cup of suffering." (See Matthew 26:39, 42; Luke 22:42.) The thought of the cross was unbearable to handle alone. He asked three of His closest disciples to pray with Him. With His face to the ground, Jesus agonized in prayer. He was in such turmoil that His *sweat was like drops of blood falling to the ground* (Luke 22:44). It was not enough for Him to pray once; He felt the need to pray a second time for the same thing. Again, He pleaded with the Father to take away the cup, but He also expressed His willingness to do whatever the Father willed Him to do. *"My Father, if it is not possible for this cup to be taken away unless I drink it, may your will be done"* (Matthew 26:42). After He had prayed a third time (see verse 44), He felt at peace. An angel appeared and strengthened Him. (See Luke 22:43.) Finally, He was ready to obey and die on the cross for our sins.

If you measure the effectiveness of Jesus' prayers for the cup to be taken away by their outcome, then you would call them a failure—God did not remove the cup, did He? However, if you consider that Jesus was assuredly also asking for the strength to obey His heavenly Father, then you can say that His prayers were answered. The purpose of His prayers was not to change His circumstances but to change Himself. He felt weak and in need of strength. Jesus' prayers were answered in that He received the strength and power He needed. As a result, He was able to drink the full cup of God's wrath and complete the act of redemption on our behalf.

Jesus Prays a Prayer of Faith

Contrast the above prayer of submission with a prayer of faith. One day, Jesus rebuked a fig tree for not bearing fruit. (See Mark 11:12–14.) The next day, the disciples noticed that the tree had withered. (See Mark 11:20–21.) Without batting an eye, Jesus said, *"I tell you the truth, if anyone says to this mountain, 'Go, throw yourself into the sea,' and does not doubt in his heart but believes that what he says will happen, it will be done for him"* (Mark 11:23). Then, He added this simple truth about the prayer of faith: *"Therefore I tell you, whatever you ask for in prayer, believe that you have received it, and it will be yours"* (Mark 11:24). Notice the confidence in this type of prayer. Jesus told His disciples to count the thing as done, even if they did not see any results immediately after praying. Just as there were no immediate results after Jesus cursed the fig tree, the results of your prayers of faith may take some time to manifest. Don't look at the "tree"; just understand that the answer has been given and will manifest in time.

The purpose of the prayer of faith is to move mountains—in other words, to knock down any obstacle that stands in the way of God's will, whether sickness, lack of money, confusion, or something else. If you pray in faith, that mountain *will* move—that's the proof of the prayer's success. Again, the purpose of the prayer of faith is different from the purpose of the prayer of submission. This is a prayer meant to bring about a change in circumstances.

Again, in the garden of Gethsemane, Jesus prayed not once but three times. Some people invoke this fact to support the belief that when you ask God to heal you, you need to keep asking again and again, until He does it. But that rule does not apply to the prayer of faith. Jesus said, *"Believe you have received it"* (Mark 11:24). If you believe you have received the thing you asked for, you do not need to keep asking for it over and over again. Doing so reveals a lack of belief.

When Jesus rebuked the fig tree, He did it only once, with no repeats. That's because it was a prayer of faith. Yet, when He prayed in the garden of Gethsemane, He kept praying until He was strengthened. That's because it was a prayer of submission. You should keep on praying when you find yourself in need of strength to overcome weakness and temptation.

Mistake #2: Doubting the Will of God

As we have seen, another mistake people make when they pray is misappropriating the phrase *"Yet not as I will, but as you will*" (Matthew 26:39). For example, a pastor might pray, "Lord, help our church to grow. Bring in more people who need to be saved. Yet not our will but Your will be done." What pastor, in his right mind, wonders whether God desires his church to grow and to draw more lost souls to Christ? Success in evangelism is God's will for every pastor, church, and ministry. So, in a prayer of this nature, there is no need to use the phrase "Not my will but Yours be done."

On the other hand, when God calls you to do something you do not feel comfortable doing, yet you desire to obey Him, you would do well to pray, "Not my will but Yours be done."

Mistake #3: Confusing the Prayer of Petition with the Prayer of Intercession

Another common error is confusing the prayer of petition with the prayer of intercession. We have these instructions from the apostle Paul: *"Do not be anxious about anything, but in everything, by prayer and petition, with thanksgiving, present your requests to God"* (Philippians 4:6). If your petition is a personal request, then your prayer should be simple. God has promised to meet all your needs (see Philippians 4:19), and so, if you ask Him for something, one request is sufficient. After that, quit worrying about it! There is no need to continue petitioning God for the same request.

However, if you are praying on behalf of someone else— also known as "interceding"—you may need to continue praying for that person. The reason is simple: if the person for whom you are praying does not believe he has received the thing you are praying for, then the instructions given in Mark 11:24, which relate primarily to prayers for personal

COMMON MISTAKES PRAYING PEOPLE MAKE 135

needs, do not apply. In Mark 11:24, Jesus said, *"What things soever ye desire, when ye pray, believe that ye receive them, and ye shall have them"* (Mark 11:24 KJV). Jesus was talking about prayers for the things that *"ye desire."* He was not talking about prayers for the desires and needs of others. Let's say that a friend of yours is considering leaving his wife. If this is his intention, then he is not about to pray for the strength to stay with her. It's up to you to pray that he will see the error in his ways and remain faithful to his marriage vows. However, it's up to him to believe that he has received this strength. You cannot do that for him. Therefore, you need to persevere with prayers of intercession on his behalf, asking God to change his heart until it happens.

When you pray for others, keep in mind that they still have free will. Your prayers may move them into a position where they have an opportunity to decide, by their own will, to obey God. However, no amount of praying can force those people into obeying God and walking in His perfect will for their lives. Again, this is why you may need to repeat your intercessory prayers until the people for whom you are praying undergo change.

Let us remember, therefore, that the rules of intercessory prayer are different from those that govern personal petitions. For example, in Paul's intercession for the believers in the Ephesian church, he said, *"I keep asking that the God of our Lord Jesus Christ, the glorious Father, may give you…"* (Ephesians 1:17). He did not ask once but kept on praying for them.

Personal petitions may receive answers more readily because the person who prays desires the answer; he or she believes in faith for the answer. However, as we have seen, with intercessory prayer, the person being prayed for may not desire the same outcome as the person who is praying and certainly may not have the same commitment to God—if any. Therefore, there is no guarantee of getting answers when you pray for others.

If there were a guarantee, then why didn't Paul offer it to the spouses of unbelievers? Instead, he said, *"How do you know, wife, whether you will save your husband? Or, how do you know, husband, whether you will save your wife?"* (1 Corinthians 7:16). Again, unbelievers have free will and, consequently, may choose to reject God. Do not get discouraged over this statement, for Paul also promised, *"For the unbelieving husband has been sanctified through his wife, and the unbelieving wife has been sanctified through her believing husband"* (1 Corinthians 7:14). This means that your faith and prayers can promote a work in the heart of an unbeliever, whether it's a spouse, another family member, or a friend. However, there is no guarantee, for that person must make a personal decision in order to be saved.

There is one other thing to note about the prayer of intercession. While it is true that all of us need others praying for us, God expects all of us to mature to the point where we depend less on the prayers of others, because we have learned to pray for ourselves.

When we were first saved, during our spiritual "infancy," most of us depended heavily on the prayers of other people. You might remember how often you sought the prayers of your pastor. You probably went forward every time he gave a call for prayer, and it may have seemed that God answered every prayer that was made on your behalf. However, God expects you to grow and learn to depend on your own prayers, just as a mother who nurses and feeds her infant child expects him to grow and one day feed himself.

You may find that the prayers of others on your behalf begin to lose their effectiveness as you mature in your walk with God. This is because He wants you to develop your own prayer life.

Famed healing evangelist and university founder Oral Roberts once took a survey of the people he had prayed for. The survey results showed that those who were not acquainted with him and his healing ministry were more likely to be healed than those who had been brought up in a church that taught divine healing. You would have expected the opposite. I believe the explanation is simple: *"From everyone who has been given much, much will be demanded"* (Luke 12:48). We are responsible for obeying and walking in the biblical principles we have been taught.

I received an e-mail from a middle-aged man who said that he did not believe God existed. He based this conclusion on something that had occurred early in his Christian walk: he had prayed for his grandmother to be healed, and yet she died. Because his prayer was not answered, he concluded that God does not exist. In his reasoning, this man committed a grave error: he assumed that intercession works the same way as personal petition.

Not every person I pray for receives an answer. But I don't allow that to weaken my faith in God's power to answer prayer. He has *always* answered my personal petitions, but I have no way of forcing those for whom I pray to believe they have received that for which I am interceding.

It is not enough for someone to consent to my praying for him. If that person does not believe along with me, then his doubts may negate the effect of my prayers. I have seen this happen many times. If those for whom you pray do not exercise their own faith, it is likely that your prayers on their behalf will return null and void.

Even Jesus' prayers for healing were nullified when He came to His hometown, where *"he did not do many miracles… because of their lack of faith"* (Matthew 13:58). The doubts of others can affect your prayers, which is why you need to increase your intercessory prayers until the doubt has vanished.

Mistake #4: Confusing the Prayer of Deliverance with the Prayer of Binding and Loosing

Prayers of deliverance are similar to prayers of binding and loosing. Some people even think they are one and the same. But they are not. The prayer of deliverance was mentioned in the Great Commission, when Jesus said, *"In my name they will drive out demons"* (Mark 16:17). If you are truly possessed by a demon, you cannot drive it out from yourself; someone else must do it for you. The participation of someone else on your behalf makes prayers of deliverance similar to prayers of intercession.

Some people may try to get someone else to cast out a demon from them, never realizing that their problem is not demon possession but demonic thoughts. These two issues are entirely separate, as are the methods of dealing with them. If a demon actually indwells a person, someone else must pray a prayer of deliverance in order to cast it out. There is no such thing as "self-deliverance."

I receive many letters and e-mails such as the one I got from Jeff, who wanted to know how he could tell that he had been delivered from demon possession. He told me that, for the last ten years, he had practiced self-deliverance. At first, someone prayed for him and cast out demons. He felt good for a few months, and then, a nagging thought came to him: *You are not really free.* So, he attempted to cast the demons out of himself. He began to feel certain demons working inside his body. He wrote, "Sometimes, I feel demons in my hands; other times, I feel them in my throat. They roam around in my body."

The problem was that Jeff was using the wrong prayer for his situation. Jeff did not suffer from demon possession but from demonic thoughts. God began showing me how the devil works through both demon possession and demonic thoughts. I realized that, while prayers of deliverance were effective for demon possession, the expulsion of demonic thoughts requires a prayer of binding and loosing.

The prayer of binding and loosing is more akin to personal petitions in that you pray it on your own behalf. Jesus said, *"I tell you the truth, whatever you bind on earth will be bound in heaven, and whatever you loose on earth will be loosed in heaven"* (Matthew 18:18). You have the power to bind the devil and loose angels in your own life.

In the kingdom of God, there is an ongoing battle between God and Satan, between angels and demons. Jesus explained it like this:

> *The kingdom of heaven is like a man who sowed good seed in his field. But while everyone was sleeping, his enemy came and sowed weeds among the wheat, and went away. When the wheat sprouted and formed heads, then the weeds also appeared.* (Matthew 13:24–26)

God and Satan alike sow seeds: God sows His Word, and Satan sows his "word"—deception and falsehood. The *"field"* Jesus spoke of is your heart. God works at changing your life by sowing His Word into your heart, and the result is that you produce spiritual fruit. Meanwhile, in his efforts to stifle the growth of spiritual fruit in your life, Satan sows his word—his lies and falsehoods—into your heart in an effort to make weeds grow there. These weeds, if left alone, will stifle the Word of God and rob you of a harvest of spiritual fruit.

God gave me a revelation based on the above passage. The enemy, after sowing weeds, *"went away."* He did not even stay to watch the weeds grow. He left. God spoke to me and said, *Tom, sometimes My people think the devil is personally with them in the form of demons. Most of the time, the devil is not still there, but his weeds still grow, making My children believe that they have a demon.*

Wow! I was beginning to understand how demons work. In some cases, demons actually inhabit people, and the only solution is deliverance, through a prayer of deliverance. Someone who knows his authority in Christ can cast out demons from other people. However, if the problem is not the presence of a demon but rather a demonic thought, and if the person does not realize this, he may go through hundreds of deliverance sessions and never feel free. Again, the reason is that, while a demon-possessed person requires someone else to drive out his demons, someone suffering from demonic thoughts is the only one who can cast out those thoughts. People like Jeff do not need deliverance; they need to weed out the seeds sown in their minds by the devil.

COMMON MISTAKES PRAYING PEOPLE MAKE 141

This is when it's time for a prayer of binding and loosing. You bind the devil by pulling down the *"imaginations"* (2 Corinthians 10:5) that he tricked you into accepting as real. You need to use your authority and bind the devil by speaking the Word of God.

Jesus did not have a demon when He was tempted in the desert. But the devil tried to plant thoughts in His mind, which He refused. As we have seen, He bound Satan in two ways. First, He spoke Scripture, saying several times, *"It is written...."* (See, for example, Matthew 4:4, 7, 10.) You do not win the battle for your mind by dwelling on the thoughts the devil planted there. You win it by speaking God's Word. Second, Jesus said, *"Away from me, Satan!"* (Matthew 4:10). This was not an instance of self-deliverance. This was Jesus taking His authority and driving the devil away from Him.

You might say, "I tried doing that, but the devil would not leave." If that's the case, it must be that you continued thinking the thoughts that the devil planted in your mind. If you would have ignored those thoughts or, better yet, cast them out, then the devil could not have managed to remain with you, in your head. You gave him permission to stay because you would not believe the Word of God. Don't argue and insist, "But I *do* believe God's Word." No, you don't. If the devil is still messing with your mind, then you have given him the right to do so, through your wrong thoughts.

The solution is not to get someone to pray for you. The solution is to bind the devil by ridding your mind of his thoughts. And you do this through a prayer of binding and loosing.

Anna Discovers the Power of Binding and Loosing

It was a prayer of binding and loosing that Anna needed to speak. She had flown all the way from Canada to visit my church in Texas. Having seen me on television and hearing about my deliverance ministry, she believed that if anyone could deliver her from her demons, I could.

I met her for the first time during our Sunday morning service. Her Italian accent was unmistakable. She was in her sixties, but she looked young for her age. Her personality was absolutely sweet. She enjoyed the service and asked if she could meet with me on Monday morning. I agreed.

On Monday, she came to my office, accompanied by her daughter. Anna explained that she had suffered from demon possession for many years. She said she even heard voices.

After listening to her story, I said to her, "Anna, what wicked things do the demons make you do?"

She looked puzzled. "What do you mean?"

"Do they make you commit adultery?"

She gasped. "Oh no, I have never committed adultery against my husband."

"Okay, do they make you get drunk?"

"No, I do not drink."

"Well then, what wicked or unclean things do the demons within you make you do?"

She could not think of anything bad that she had been doing.

Then, her daughter spoke up. "Oh, Pastor, my mother is the sweetest person I know. She is the most godly person

I know; she doesn't do anything wrong. She is a saint. And God knows she has every reason to be bitter toward my father, but she always treats him with respect and is kind to everyone."

I smiled. "You made my point. You see, from the first time I met Anna, I knew she did not have a demon." I looked at Anna and said, "Sister, if a demon really was inside of you, then the demon would make you do evil things. The fact that you live a holy life is proof that you do not have a demon. What you do have is a demonic thought that has condemned you. The devil has told you for a long time that you are sinful and evil, and you have been believing his lies. You feel that you are not forgiven, so the devil takes advantage of your guilt. This is why you hear voices. You need to stop the devil by speaking positive Scriptures about God's love for you."

I taught her how to pull down imaginations, and I said a powerful prayer over her. But I did not pray to cast out any demons, especially because doing so would only have reinforced her belief that she was possessed by a demon.

Anna was pleasantly surprised to learn that she was not demon-possessed. "Pastor," she said, "every minister that has prayed for me has always tried to cast out demons from me, but nothing has ever worked. You are the first minister that told me I did not need deliverance but simply needed to stop the lies in my mind. I am so grateful to you that you freed me with the truth."

One month later, I received an e-mail from Anna, saying, "Pastor, I no longer hear the voices. Sometimes, I struggle a little, but not like before. Thank you so much for showing me how to be free."

Many believers are struggling like Anna was, always trying to get others to pray for their deliverance from demons, when what they really need is to pray a prayer of binding and loosing.

Part III

Steps to Answered Prayer

Chapter 13

Step One: Think Big with God

Our Father which art in heaven....
—Matthew 6:9 KJV

The first truth Jesus taught about prayer is that we pray to a God who dwells in heaven, not on earth. This does not mean that God is far away from us but that He is *beyond* us. He is transcendent. *Transcendent* is a big theological word that simply means God is beyond the limitations of this world. He created the earth, but He is not bound by its laws and rules. He can do more than natural laws allow.

The law of gravity does not permit a body of water to separate into two walls, but God achieved this very thing at the Red Sea because of Moses' faith. (See Exodus 14:21–22.) The law of rotation does not allow the sun to stop in one place, but God did this at Joshua's request. (See Joshua 10:12–13.) The law of seed time and harvest does not allow for water to turn into wine, but Jesus performed this act at a wedding at the behest of His mother, Mary. (See John 2:1–11.) The beginning of prayer is to recognize that you are not praying to a God of this earth but to your heavenly Father, who is greater than any earthly law. To put it simply, there is no limit to what prayer can do. You do not pray merely for what is *possible* but for what is *impossible*.

146

"Now to him who is able to do immeasurably more than all we ask or imagine, according to his power that is at work within us" (Ephesians 3:20). This passage has been misinterpreted to mean that when you pray for something, God will give you something far beyond what you asked for or imagined. That sounds good, but the apostle Paul was only stating the obvious: that God is bigger than anything you might imagine Him giving you. It is not that God will give you more, but rather that He is *"able"* to give you more. He will, however, give you what you ask.

"Ask and it will be given to you" (Luke 11:9). If you do not ask, you will not receive. This means that we are the ones who limit the blessings God will bestow. The psalmist confirmed this truth: *"Yea, they turned back and tempted God, and limited the Holy One of Israel"* (Psalm 78:41 KJV). Even though the Israelites had been assured by God that they would enter the Promised Land, they did not possess it immediately. In fact, the first generation failed to enter the Promised Land *"because of their unbelief"* (Hebrews 3:19). It took the Israelites forty years to finally realize their potential and enter into the promise of God. Like the Israelites, we often waive the blessings of God because of our own unbelief.

It should not surprise us that we limit God's response to our prayers. Remember, when Jesus tried to heal the people in His hometown, Scripture tells us that He *"did not do many miracles there because of their lack of faith"* (Matthew 13:58). The people of Nazareth limited the power of Christ, and we often do the same thing when we pray.

Unleash Your Imagination

A couple was taking a tour of the most beautiful residences in Nantucket. When the tour bus stopped at the largest mansion in the area, the couple got off the bus and began taking pictures of the gorgeous home. As they snapped a few shots, the husband turned to his wife and said, "I can't imagine living in a house like this." Just then, the Holy Spirit spoke to his heart, saying, *Then, you will never live in a house like this.*

The man wondered, *What do You mean?*

Then, he felt God's reply: *If you cannot imagine it, you cannot have it.*

The man repented and then said to his wife, "I *can* imagine God giving us a house like this. He is a big God!"

This man had realized the first step in receiving the full blessing of God: thinking big. You need to expand your vision of God and see Him as bigger than whatever it is you lack.

You Set the Borders

God spoke to Abram, saying, *"Lift up your eyes from where you are and look north and south, east and west. All the land that you see I will give to you and your offspring forever"* (Genesis 13:14–15). God promised to give Abram everything he could "see." If he could not see it, then it would not be his. In other words, Abram determined the borders of the land he would possess. Whatever he saw, he could have.

God also encouraged Abram not to limit his possession by standing still. God challenged him, *"Go, walk through the length and breadth of the land, for I am giving it to you"* (Genesis 13:17). God was encouraging Abram to increase his vision.

Just like Abram, you need to think bigger. Don't just stay where you are; go beyond where your feet are planted and walk the land to see more of your property. Abram was a surveyor, laying stakes to his possession with his eyes. You can do the same thing. Whatever you can imagine, that is your border. That is your possession.

Jesus said, *"If therefore thine eye be single, thy whole body shall be full of light"* (Matthew 6:22 KJV). In essence, the eyes of the mind and heart—the imagination—are the light of the body. What you see moves you. What you see inspires you. If you see lack and problems, then the eyes are dark, and you cannot imagine anything good. But, if you will turn on the light within you and begin to see success, then you can seize it.

Everything is created twice: first in your mind, and then in the world. The first creation is primary. Nothing ever comes into being unless it is first created in the mind. God first thought of creation and then went to work creating it. If you cannot see the blessings in your mind, you will not be able to see them in your world.

"I Had Walked That Runway a Thousand Times Before"

Like many little girls, Tara Dawn Holland watched the Miss America Pageant devotedly. As a child, she would pretend to be Miss America by tying a beach towel around her body and walking the halls of her home. In seventh grade, she attended a concert of former Miss America Cheryl Pruitt. Cheryl autographed a copy of her biography for Tara.

At school, Tara's teacher required the students to read a biography and give an oral presentation on it. Naturally, Tara chose the biography of Cheryl Pruitt. On the day of her presentation, she stood before her class dressed just like the subject of her presentation, wearing a "Miss America" sash and a crown she'd made from a cardboard box, overlaid with foil and sprinkled with glitter. She addressed her classmates proudly, saying, "Good morning. I'm Miss America." This was her vision and her passion.

Later, Tara competed twice in the Miss Florida Pageant, placing second both times. Hoping a new location would make the difference, she moved to Kansas, entered the competition there, and won! Later that year, Tara Dawn Holland was crowned Miss America. She walked the runway with confidence. Afterward, a reporter asked her if she had been nervous. She replied, "No, because I had walked that runway a thousand times before." Of course, she was referring to the countless times she'd dreamed about becoming Miss America while walking the halls of her home.

Like Tara, I, too, had a dream. I envisioned myself not as Mr. Universe but as an apostle of miracles. Many times, I would conduct great miracle crusades—in the privacy of my own bedroom, where the audience consisted of a few action figures I'd kept from my childhood. I remember preaching and calling the multitudes to come forward for prayer. I saw myself laying hands on the sick and hearing their testimonies of healings. I looked foolish, no doubt, but it was my dream. I saw it. It was my call!

Today, when people see the results of my miracle ministry—blind eyes opening, the lame leaping for joy, demons being cast out—they often wonder how I seem to conduct these services with such ease. My answer is similar to Tara's. I have seen myself doing this a thousand times before.

What can you see yourself doing? What do you see yourself having? Who do you see yourself becoming?

What you see is your border; it is what you will have.

"Set the Table" for Whatever You Are Praying For

Gavin MacLeod is famous for his television roles as Murray Slaughter on *The Mary Tyler Moore Show* and Captain Merrill Stubing on *The Love Boat*. During the years *The Love Boat* was being filmed, Gavin abandoned and later divorced his wife, Patti. He fell for a cult leader and joined her movement. Patti, on the other hand, came to Christ. At a Hollywood prayer meeting, she learned how to pray successfully. She learned to believe God for the impossible. She began to pray for Gavin's salvation and for the restoration of their marriage.

Gavin began to feel remorse for what he had done. One day, he showed up at Patti's house. When she let him in, he was surprised to see two dinner plates at the table. He wondered if she was expecting someone. "Yes," she told him. "I am expecting you, Gavin." She'd never let go of her hope for a miracle. In her mind's eye, she saw the day when Gavin would return home. She acted out her faith by always setting a place for him at the dinner table.

Gavin and Patti have since remarried and have served the Lord together for many years.

Take the Limits Off of Your Thinking

Maybe you would say to me, "Pastor, I just do not have much faith."

It is not the amount of faith, but how you *use* the little faith you have, that matters. Jesus said that a mustard-seed-sized amount of faith could move mountains. (See Matthew 17:20; Luke 17:6.) So, again, it is not how much you have but what you do with it that counts. You need to learn to think big, even in seemingly limited circumstances.

I grew up in a relatively modest home, and you might have even considered my family poor. When God called me into the ministry, I wasn't expecting much money to come my way. So, when I proposed marriage to my wife, Sonia, I also gave her a reality check. Instead of promising her the moon and stars, I projected a future of sacrifice. I said, "Before you agree to marry me, understand that if God calls me to Africa, we might not have the cleanest of places to live in. If He calls me to India, we might live in roach-infested regions."

She replied, "I don't care. I love you, and I will go where you go. If I have to get a gallon of Clorox and wash the houses in which we live, I will do it."

We were married on August 13, 1983, in Fort Worth, Texas. The next day, we headed for El Paso to search for an apartment. (We'd decided it would be more fun to wait until after the wedding ceremony to find a place to live.)

I took Sonia to the "bad part" of El Paso, where it was cheaper to live. The first place we looked at was a decrepit, two-story redbrick apartment. The landlord looked like an old grizzly bear. He was smoking a cigar, and his stained white T-shirt was so short that it exposed his navel. With a gravelly voice, he barked, "What do you want?"

"Uh, we saw an ad for an apartment," I replied.

Bothered, he said, "Follow me."

He took us to the second floor and opened a squeaky, beaten wooden door. "Here it is," he said, matter-of-factly.

The musty apartment consisted in a single room that was designed to function as living room, bedroom, and kitchen—if the portable heating stove on the counter qualified as a cooking instrument.

Terror began to descend upon my new bride. "Let's keep looking," she said.

Next, I took her under the freeway to an old, nearly abandoned apartment complex. The thousands of cars passing overhead made a deafening noise. Once again, she said, "Let's keep looking." Our "fun" search was turning into a torturous quest. Sonia was not happy with anything we saw.

After we'd looked at several more pitiful apartments, she said, "Tom, God is bigger than this!"

I agreed, but I couldn't help thinking, *But my wallet isn't!*

When Sonia told my mother about all the places we had seen, my mother scolded me and said, "Tom, you cannot take Sonia to those places. They're dangerous. You need to look in the nice part of town."

The next day, despite my reluctance, I took Sonia to the more affluent side of town. The first apartment we saw was clean and nicely furnished, with a comfortable living room, a separate kitchen, a spacious bedroom, and a spotless bathroom. Immediately, she said, "We'll take it!"

I wanted to say, "Wait a minute. How much is it?" Instead, I agreed and put down a deposit.

I did not know how we were going to pay for the apartment. I did not have great faith. My faith was no bigger than a tiny mustard seed. However, mustard seeds grow to become large trees. So, I planted my seeds of faith in prayer and decided to trust God to help us pay for the apartment. And He did. Not once did we fall behind in our payments. God was faithful to supply all our needs.

You may feel as dubious as I did about stepping out in faith. You do not have to be overly endowed with a special gift of faith in order for miracles to happen in your life. You just need to plant a seed of faith in prayer and then wait for it to grow. Maybe you decide to write a book when no one is wanting to publish it. Maybe you start a church when there are few people expressing interest in attending. Maybe you record a music album when there is no audience anxious to buy it. Maybe you start a business with little capital. Steps of faith such as these demonstrate your belief in a big God.

You need to get out of your "barely-getting-by" mentality. Think big. Think increase. Think abundance. Think more than enough. Think maximum living.

Envision the Fulfillment of Your Prayers

There is an old story about a professional golfer from the U.S. who was invited to play golf with the king of Arabia for an entire week. The king put him up in a beautiful resort with a full-time butler at his service. The golfer's every need was met. When the week ended, the king told him that it was the custom of his country to give his guests a gift.

The golfer was touched but replied, "Your Highness, I am honored just to be invited. It is not necessary to give me anything."

The king insisted, "I would be very offended if you did not allow me to give you a gift."

Thinking on his feet, the golfer said, "Well, a nice golf club would be fine."

Shortly after returning to the States, the golfer received a package in the mail from the king of Arabia. The package was so small and lightweight, he doubted it contained a golf club. When he opened the package, he discovered a packet of legal papers. It was the title to a five-hundred-acre "golf club."

Although this story is a legend, it contains a great truth. Just as the king of Arabia thought bigger than the golfer, so, too, God thinks bigger than we do. He wants to do so much more for us than we dare to dream. We need to quit limiting Him and let Him work miracles in our lives!

The first step toward getting your prayers answered is imagining their fulfillment.

God Is Not Throwing You Away

Jerry had lost almost everything. The government had forced him to close his business and file for bankruptcy. He and his wife sold their house and moved in with friends. They were depressed, and they couldn't see how God could ever come through in their lives. I gave Jerry a prophecy: "God is not angry with you. He is not throwing you away. God is going to turn everything around in your life."

With tears streaming down his face, Jerry put what little faith he had into God's hands and asked for His blessing. God gave him a business opportunity, but Jerry had no money to invest in it. After exhausting every resource he could think of, he finally managed to scrape together a down payment. The new business took off. It was as if Jerry had been made for this new venture. With the income the new business brought in, Jerry and his wife were able to purchase a gorgeous home—worlds nicer than their previous dwelling—near the church.

Jerry is a great example of what to do when you are down in the faith department. When times are tough, pick yourself up and remember that you have a heavenly Father who is more than enough. He is not through with you. He is not throwing you away. No matter your circumstances, you need to imagine God coming through for you.

- You may have been sick for a long time, but imagine living without pain.

- You may have had marriage problems for years, but imagine being happily married.

- Your church may have stagnated over the past decade, but imagine a revival igniting there and drawing hundreds of new believers into the kingdom.

- Your business may have lost customers in the latest recession, but imagine getting them back, along with many more new customers.

- Your children may have been "prodigals" for a long time, but imagine them returning to the Lord and serving Him faithfully.

- You may have struggled financially all your life, but imagine having enough money to meet—and even exceed—every need.

Friend, the first step is to reject discouragement and to begin imagining the ways in which God is going to provide you with an abundant life. (See John 10:10.) He is as close as your prayer. What can you imagine God doing for you? Ask Him!

Chapter 14

Step Two: Depend on Christ's Merits

Hallowed be thy name.
—Matthew 6:9 KJV

In these four famous words is hidden the secret to answered prayer: God alone is holy; therefore, answered prayer is based on His holiness, not yours. Jesus emphasized this point when He told His disciples, *"I tell you the truth, my Father will give you whatever you ask **in my name**. Until now you have not asked for anything in my name. Ask and you will receive, and your joy will be complete"* (John 16:23–24). Prayer is directed to God the Father, always in the name of Jesus.

The reason we use the name of Jesus is because of His role as the *"one mediator between God and men"* (1 Timothy 2:5). We need a mediator because we are unworthy to approach God on our own merits. We cannot expect to receive answers to prayers because we believe to have been "holy" or "good." Of course, we should try to live lives that are holy and good, but our confidence in our prayers is based solely on Christ being holy in our place.

Years ago, I worked at a pizza parlor. One day, I was replenishing the salad bar with another employee named Dixie

157

when she started rubbing her leg. "Oh, Tom," she wailed, "my leg hurts so badly." Without hesitation, I laid hands on her leg and said, "In the name of Jesus, be healed." Then, I walked away.

Later, she came to me and said, "Tom, something strange happened when you prayed for me. My leg froze up in the air. What was that?"

I replied, "How is your leg?"

"Oh, the pain is gone."

"What you felt was the power of God."

Then, she proceeded to tell me how often she prayed. "Oh, I believe in prayer," she insisted. "I pray every day."

"Dixie," I said, "give me a sample of how you pray."

She said, "Well, I say something like, 'God, could You help me with school?' or whatever I need Him to help me with."

"Do you ever say, 'In the name of Jesus'?"

"No, I don't think so."

"Well, Dixie, I hate to tell you this, but God isn't going to respond to your prayers."

She was shocked. She couldn't believe I would say something like that. I explained how we are unholy and sinful from birth, and, therefore, unable to approach God without a mediator. After I had given her a full explanation, she agreed that she needed to pray in the name of Jesus.

Again, the phrase "in the name of Jesus" is not a magic incantation or a secret code; it is intended to demonstrate our need of a mediator—Someone to stand in our place and represent us before God. Jesus' statement to this effect is even more vivid in *The Living Bible*: "*You can go directly to the Father and ask him, and he will give you what you ask for because you use my name*" (John 16:23 TLB). Here, we find the reason God will give you what you ask: because you use the name of His Son, Jesus.

Using the Name of Jesus

What does it mean to use Jesus' name? Jesus explained, "*Then you will present your petitions over my signature!*" (John 16:26 TLB). The picture He used here is of someone endorsing a check to you and telling you to fill in any amount and then cash it.

What amount do you write? Are you limited by the amount in your personal account? No, because the check you are cashing does not have your signature, nor is it going to be cashed from your account! The only limit is the amount of wealth that belongs to the person who signed the check.

Trust in the Worth of Jesus

The great Christian author E. W. Kenyon was giving a discourse on the name of Jesus when a lawyer interrupted him. "Excuse me, Brother Kenyon," the man said. "I am an attorney. Based on what you are saying, has Jesus given us the power of attorney?"

Kenyon had never thought of it like that. "You are an attorney; I'm only a minister," he responded. "Tell me your opinion: has Jesus given us the power of attorney?"

The lawyer looked over the verses once more, and then said, "Well, if words mean anything, then Jesus definitely gave us the power of attorney."

"What does that mean?" Kenyon asked.

"It all depends on how wealthy the person is who gave the power of attorney. You can only act in his place using his wealth. If the man is wealthy, then you can cash a lot of checks."

At that point, it hit Kenyon: the secret to answered prayer is found in depending on the wealth and worthiness of Christ.

This revelation is absolutely essential to understand if we are to have confidence in prayer, because the enemy will try to attack us with feelings of unworthiness. He will say things like, "How can you expect God to listen to your prayers when you smoke (or drink, or cuss, or think bad thoughts)?" He will try to get you to depend on your name, which is without merit, in order to hinder your prayers. Do not fall for his schemes! Depend on Christ's good name and His vast worth.

Rest on the Righteousness of Jesus

The opposite problem also can occur. Sometimes, a person feels worthy to get answers to his prayers because he pays his tithes, he helps others, and he is a faithful spouse. Because of his "good deeds," he fully expects God to answer his prayers.

This type of thinking is absurd, as Jesus illustrated in this parable:

> *Two men went up to the temple to pray, one a Pharisee and the other a tax collector. The Pharisee stood up and prayed about himself: "God, I thank you that I am not like other men—robbers, evildoers, adulterers—or even like this tax collector. I fast twice a week and give a tenth*

of all I get." But the tax collector stood at a distance. He would not even look up to heaven, but beat his breast and said, "God, have mercy on me, a sinner." I tell you that this man, rather than the other, went home justified before God. For everyone who exalts himself will be humbled, and he who humbles himself will be exalted.

(Luke 18:10–14)

The one who had his prayers answered was the cheating tax collector who asked for mercy. The Greek word translated as "*mercy*" means "to expiate [atone], make propitiation for." The tax collector was appealing to the One who would die in his place and atone for his sins. Jesus was giving us a preview of the meaning of His death. He was revealing that the person who relies on his own works to reach God's ear will fail, but the one who relies on Christ's work of mercy on the cross will find his or her prayers answered.

Rev. Kenneth Hagin told the story of a woman who attended church faithfully, yet never seemed to receive answers to the prayers Hagin prayed on her behalf. After a while, she complained to Hagin, saying, "I have a very difficult question to ask you, Brother Hagin. Why is it that when you pray for me, God never answers? Yet Sister _____, who rarely attends church, always gets her prayers answered when you pray for her. Why does God do this?"

Rev. Hagin answered, "Oh, sister, I thought you were asking a difficult question. You see, Sister _____ may not be as faithful a Christian as you, but she has a good heart and is always confident that God will answer prayer. You, on the other hand, are a faithful Christian, yet you are prideful in your works and look down at others, and when I pray for you, you have little confidence that God will answer."

Hagin hit at the heart of the matter. There are two types of believers: those who are confident in their own righteousness and those who are confident in Christ's righteousness.

When I was a new believer, God spoke to me, saying, *Tom, stretch out your hands.* I did, and then He said, *Whenever you lay hands on the sick in My name, I will lay hands on them with you.* He was not giving me a special gift that others do not have; rather, He was showing me that when I use the name of Jesus in praying for people, it is the same as having Christ do the work. I am depending on Christ, not myself.

Jesus said, "*You may ask me for anything in my name, and I will do it*" (John 14:14). He promises to be the One healing the sick or casting out demons when we make use of His name.

Respect the Authority of Jesus

You need to have a revelation of the value of the name of Jesus. It is not enough to act like a parrot by repeating the correct words; you have to know what it means to pray in Jesus' name. That name is your authority, just as a police badge represents the law an officer is charged with enforcing. Any police officer knows that there is no magic in the badge, but he carries it at all times because it has been entrusted to him. Of course, the badge does not give him the right to abuse his authority. He is a servant of the people.

Now, someone might obtain a phony badge and act like a police officer, but that would not give him any real authority to enforce the law. The only reason anyone would impersonate an officer would not be to help others but to get something for himself.

There is a story in the Bible that illustrates the futility of trying to impersonate a true disciple of Christ.

Some Jews who went around driving out evil spirits tried to invoke the name of the Lord Jesus over those who were demon-possessed. They would say, "In the name of Jesus, whom Paul preaches, I command you to come out." Seven sons of Sceva, a Jewish chief priest, were doing this. One day the evil spirit answered them, "Jesus I know, and I know about Paul, but who are you?" Then the man who had the evil spirit jumped on them and overpowered them all. He gave them such a beating that they ran out of the house naked and bleeding.

(Acts 19:13–16)

These men did not "know" Christ. They did not have a personal relationship with Him. There are some "impersonators" today who think they are disciples of Christ, but they have not accepted Him as Lord and Savior and been born again. They really do not know Him.

We must understand that the badge of authority Jesus has given us—His name—carries great responsibility. It is not just a term for us to invoke in order to show off our power or throw our weight around. We are to use it in humility, remembering our charge to be a blessing to others.

A woman wrote to me and said, "Now, let me get this straight. If I say the right words, like 'in the name of Jesus,' God has to give me a husband of my choice."

I wrote back, "You have it wrong. A husband is not a prize that God gives away to the winning prayer. You need to pray to be the kind of person who will make a great wife for a wonderful man."

One of the difficulties I see in the body of Christ is a lack of people with a servant's heart. Many people are looking out only for themselves, wanting to discover how they can get all of God's blessings. They forget that we are called to love God first, others second, and ourselves third. This is what it means to use the name of Jesus. Does this mean that you shouldn't ask God for anything that pertains to you? Of course not. God loves you and wants to bless you. However, He honors the person who uses His name and knows what that really entails.

Using Jesus' Name Properly

Therefore say to the house of Israel, "This is what the Sovereign LORD *says: It is not for your sake, O house of Israel, that I am going to do these things, but for the sake of my holy name, which you have profaned among the nations where you have gone. I will show the holiness of my great name, which has been profaned among the nations, the name you have profaned among them. Then the nations will know that I am the* LORD, *declares the Sovereign* LORD, *when I show myself holy through you before their eyes."* (Ezekiel 36:22–23)

There are two important things that God points out in the above passage. First, He says that the reason He does great things in the world is because of *"the sake of* [His] *holy name."* God is good, and He honors His own name among the nations by demonstrating His goodness and holiness. Second, God is telling Israel that He will not bless the world for their sake. In fact, He explains that their name has acquired a bad reputation. He accuses them of having *"profaned"* His name. To profane God's name is to misuse it, akin to a corrupt police officer using his badge for personal gain or to harm others instead of to uphold the law.

When my father was very ill, he granted me power of attorney. However, that did not mean that he wanted me to take all his money and transfer it to my account, leaving my sister high and dry. I had the power to do that, but it would have been an abuse of the power he had granted me. The same is true when it comes to using the name of Jesus. God looks at our hearts and desires us to use Jesus' name in prayer for His kingdom, not for our own kingdoms.

Don't Misuse the Name

I see so much misuse of Jesus' name in the church. I see people misuse it in judging others. The reverse is also true, when people misuse it in advocating sinful practices. They brag about their immoral behavior, saying, "God loves me for who I am. He would never ask me to change." Listen: Jesus' name is holy, so it is senseless to insist that He will accept your sin. *He will not.*

Don't Deny the Power in the Name

Another serious abuse of the name of Jesus is denying that Christ has the same power and authority today as He had when He was on earth. There are some who believe that there was a suspension or cessation of the spiritual gifts of healing and miracles after the apostles died. These people assume—wrongly—that the powers to heal, to speak in tongues, and to cast out demons were gifts given only to the apostles, and that when they died, the gifts died with them. Those who subscribe to this view do not believe that God still performs miracles in our modern times. They dishonor Jesus' name by suggesting that it no longer has value or power, aside from a power to save the lost.

Yet, Jesus gave us the power of His name so that we might also heal the sick and cast out demons: *"And these signs will accompany those who believe: In my name they will drive out demons; they will speak in new tongues;...they will place their hands on sick people, and they will get well"* (Mark 16:17–18).

Notice that Jesus did not say that these were "apostolic signs"; He said that *"these signs will accompany those who believe."* The reason believers still walk in these signs today is that they have been given use of the name of Jesus. Jesus said, *"In my name they will...."* It is the name of Jesus that enables us to heal people and deliver them from demon possession.

The name of Jesus has not lost any of its power and authority. In fact, since Christ's exaltation to the right hand of God, His power and authority—and ours, too—have increased.

> *And being found in appearance as a man, [Jesus] humbled himself and became obedient to death—even death on a cross! Therefore God exalted him to the highest place and gave him the name that is above every name, that at the name of Jesus every knee should bow, in heaven and on earth and under the earth, and every tongue confess that Jesus Christ is Lord, to the glory of God the Father.* (Philippians 2:8–11)

While He was on the earth, Jesus had authority over sickness, demons, and nature. After His death and resurrection, He had authority over all three realms of existence: *"in heaven," "on earth,"* and *"under the earth."* After His resurrection, Jesus appeared to His disciples and said, *"All authority in heaven and on earth has been given to me"* (Matthew 28:18). Now, His name had been invested with *"all authority."*

Since Jesus is now exalted to God's right hand, we have access to even more miraculous power than before. This is what Jesus meant when He said,

> I tell you the truth, anyone who has faith in me will do what I have been doing. He will do even **greater things** than these, because I am going to the Father. And I will do whatever you ask in my name, so that the Son may bring glory to the Father.　(John 14:12–13)

We can do *"greater things."* This is not because we are greater than Jesus, but rather because Jesus is now greater than He was while on the earth. He is in heaven with greater authority, restored to His majesty, splendor, and honor.

Therefore, it is erroneous to believe that miracles passed away with the apostles. As we have seen, the truth is, we should be experiencing even greater miracles in our lives than in Jesus' time, because His name has more authority than it did before. When you pray and use Jesus' name, expect God to treat your prayers the way He would treat Christ's prayers. You will receive answers.

Chapter 15

Step Three: Stand on God's Word

Thy kingdom come. Thy will be done in earth, as it is in heaven.
—Matthew 6:10 KJV

One of the questions I pose to people who ask me to pray for them is this: "What Scripture are you standing on to guarantee that God will answer your prayer?"

The usual reply is, "Nothing in particular."

And that is what they get: *Nothing in particular.*

Our Lord is a sovereign God, which means that He is free to do whatever He wants. He answers to no one. Nobody can move God in any direction He does not want to go. He is not influenced by anybody.

You might conclude that there is no point in having any confidence that God will work in a certain way. And that would be a reasonable conclusion—if God had not bound Himself to His Word. One of the great truths of Scripture is that God is faithful to His own Word. The Bible puts it this way: *"Know therefore that the LORD your God is God; he is the faithful God, keeping his covenant of love to a thousand*

generations of those who love him and keep his commands"
(Deuteronomy 7:9).

Two things stand out in this verse. First, "God is God,"
which means that He acts without any conditions or con-
straints. No one forces Him to do anything or bars Him
from doing anything. Many believers understand this first
principle when it comes to prayer, yet they fail to understand
the second important fact: He is "the faithful God." You cannot call someone "faithful" if he does not keep his word. God
is faithful; therefore, He will fulfill that which He has promised to His children. So, while God is God and is therefore
free to do whatever He wants, He has bound Himself to His
people through His Word so that they may depend on Him.

God's Will Is Not a Mystery

The statement "Thy will be done in earth, as it is in heaven"
(Matthew 6:10 KJV) is connected with God's sovereignty and
faithfulness—and not one more than the other. So, when we
declare, "God's will be done," that doesn't mean we have no
idea of God's will. Rather, it means that we are counting on
God to provide something He has already promised to us.
God's will is tied to His Word. If God has promised in His
Word to do something for us, then we can conclude that it
must be His will. God's will is not some unknown, mysteri-
ous purpose that He keeps secret from us. Rather, He has
made His will known through His Word.

"And he made known to us the mystery of his will according to
his good pleasure, which he purposed in Christ" (Ephesians 1:9).
The mystery of God's will has been clarified for us. There is
no real confidence in prayer if you do not know the will of
God.

You might ask, "Doesn't the Bible say that God's thoughts and ways are not our thoughts and ways?" (See Isaiah 55:8.) Yes, it does. So, knowing how far we were from knowing His will, God gave us His Word.

> *As the heavens are higher than the earth, so are my ways higher than your ways and my thoughts than your thoughts....My word that goes out from my mouth... will not return to me empty, but will accomplish what I desire and achieve the purpose for which I sent it.*
>
> (Isaiah 55:9, 11)

God solved our problem of being so far from His thoughts and will by giving us His Word.

God Reveals His Will Through Jesus

The highest revelation of God's Word is Jesus, who is one with the Word: *"In the beginning was the Word, and the Word was with God, and the Word was God"* (John 1:1). Jesus is the will of God personified. Jesus said, *"I have come down from heaven not to do my will but to do the will of him who sent me"* (John 6:38). He revealed God's will not only through His teaching but also—and more important—through His actions. Jesus emphasized the ultimate purpose of His actions: *"to do...the will of him who sent me."*

This means that you can discover the will of God by observing the acts of Christ. For example, when it came to His interactions with sinners, Jesus always forgave them. Consider how quickly He forgave the prostitute who wept and, as she did, used her tears to clean His feet, wiping them with her hair. (See Luke 7:38–50.) In Jesus' eyes, no sinner was too far gone to find his way back to God.

Sandra once was a faithful woman of God, but, after divorcing her husband, she lost confidence in God's love for her. She fell back into her old habits, which included smoking. Later, however, she reconciled with her former husband, and they remarried. She wrote me, "Pastor, I want to serve God, but I still smoke. I have rid myself of everything else but the cigarettes. Is there any hope for me? Can God still use me, even if I smoke? Or do I have to stop serving Him until I am able to quit?"

While smoking is an unhealthy habit, nicotine will not stop the mercy of God. I wrote back to her, "Of course, God can still use you for His glory. You are not too far gone." In Luke 7, I believe Jesus forgave the prostitute even before she repented. The only evidence of her remorse was her shedding of tears. Sometimes, your tears are the only thing God needs to see. Sandra's letter showed her desire to live right. This was enough for God to continue to bless and use her.

God Reveals His Will Through His Word

You may think I was presumptuous to declare that God could still use Sandra as an honorable vessel. But I had the example of Christ's merciful treatment of the prostitute to help me understand God's will for her. I do not have a specific Scripture that says God still loves you if you smoke cigarettes—the Bible never mentions them—but the actions of Christ toward sinners helps me understand the will of God regarding people like Sandra.

The same goes for healing. Many people pray for good health but have little or no confidence that God's will is to heal them. They try to find Scriptures to prove God's desire to heal, when one simple way to prove His will in this regard is to observe how Christ treated the sick.

My favorite story of healing in the Bible is of the leper who came to Jesus to be cured—a story we looked at earlier. *"A man with leprosy came and knelt before him and said, 'Lord, if you are willing, you can make me clean'"* (Matthew 8:2). Remember that this man was unsure whether it was Jesus' will for him to be made well. How was this man ever going to have confidence in his prayer to Christ? There was only one way for him to have faith: Jesus was going to have to remove his doubt. *"Jesus reached out his hand and touched the man. 'I am willing,' he said. 'Be clean!' Immediately he was cured of his leprosy"* (Matthew 8:3).

Jesus was emphatic: "I am willing." Again. *The New Testament in Modern English* by J. B. Phillips translates it as, *"Of course I want to."* This makes it seem as if Jesus' feelings were hurt by the doubt of the leper—as if Jesus thought, *How dare he think I do not want to heal those who are sick? Of course, I want to heal the sick!*

I am surprised by the number of sincere believers who doubt God's willingness to heal. And yet, there are encouraging accounts of those who stand on His Word and believe in His desire to heal His children.

Melissa is the mother of twin girls. When she was twenty-one weeks into her pregnancy, the doctors discovered a low level of fluid in the amniotic sac surrounding one of the fetuses, but they said there was nothing they could do. They gave the child a 20 percent chance of surviving the delivery and a 5 percent chance of living a healthy life.

Melissa made her church family aware of the problem, and everyone began to pray. While some Christians began praying for total healing, there were others who told Melissa that maybe God's plan was for her to have only one child.

Melissa rejected those man-made arguments. She stood on the Word of God.

She started telling everyone that both of her babies were going to be healthy. It was a bold statement to make, considering the odds, but God is not concerned with percentages. He loves the underdog. He loves to show up and defy human expectations. Melissa even went so far as to name her children: Lola and Maddie. Then, her faith was really tested. For the next two weeks, the amniotic fluid decreased even more. But Melissa had a word from God. She did not give up her faith. After those two weeks, miraculously, the amniotic fluid increased dramatically. The doctors had no explanation for the rapid rise. They even agreed with Melissa that it had been an answer to prayer.

Melissa gave birth to two healthy baby girls.

It is easy to get discouraged when your faith is tested. It's easy to assume that God's will is something other than complete health. But you must hear the words of Jesus, who told the leper, "*I am willing.*" You are simply *wishing* that God will heal you; you must *know* that He is willing, because Jesus is the will of God personified.

Believing in God Versus Believing God

But Abram said, "O Sovereign LORD, what can you give me since I remain childless and the one who will inherit my estate is Eliezer of Damascus?" And Abram said, "You have given me no children; so a servant in my household will be my heir." Then the word of the LORD came to him: "This man will not be your heir, but a son coming from your own body will be your heir." He took

> him outside and said, "Look up at the heavens and count
> the stars—if indeed you can count them." Then he said
> to him, "So shall your offspring be." Abram believed the
> LORD, and he credited it to him as righteousness.
>
> (Genesis 15:2–6)

At first, Abram had no confidence that God would give
him a child. He began by asking God if there was any chance
that He would answer his request. God responded by promising Abram a son. Once God had given him the promise,
Abram *"believed the LORD."* He was not able to believe until
God had made him a promise.

Many times, people tell me, "I do believe in the Lord." So
what? Abram believed in the Lord, too, but there is a vast difference between *believing in* the Lord and *believing* the Lord.
Abram knew that nothing was too difficult for God, but that
knowledge alone was insufficient. He needed to know that
God would give him a son. Until he received God's promise, he had no such confidence. Faith is not simply accepting
God's existence; faith is accepting God's promises. Unless
you have a promise from God that your prayer will be answered, you cannot have true faith.

God gave Abram an additional promise. Not only
would God give him a child, but He would also give him the
land of Canaan: *"I am the LORD, who brought you out of Ur
of the Chaldeans to give you this land to take possession of it"*
(Genesis 15:7). In this case, however, Abram needed an additional confirmation. *"Abram said, 'O Sovereign LORD, how
can I know that I will gain possession of it?'"* (Genesis 15:8).
Abram did not have the same confidence about inheriting the
Promised Land as he did about being given a son.

We often exhibit similar doubt. We have confidence that God will heal us, but, when it comes to His material provision, great doubt overcomes us. Abram did not have a problem believing that God could heal his wife of barrenness, but it was difficult for him to believe that God would provide him with such wealth. Is that true for you, too?

It was for me. I believed in God's healing power, but when it came to finances, I was skeptical. It was difficult to believe that God wanted to prosper me. Then, one day, I took the matter to God in prayer, saying, "Lord, I hear that Your desire is to prosper me, but others say it is not true. I do not know what to believe, so I am going to read Your Word and accept whatever it teaches."

God heard my heartfelt prayer. As I searched the Scriptures, God clearly showed me that He had promised to bless me with material wealth. There were so many promises of prosperity that I could no longer ignore them.

Here is a small assortment of the promises I found:

You will have plenty to eat, until you are full, and you will praise the name of the LORD your God, who has worked wonders for you. (Joel 2:26)

The LORD will open the heavens, the storehouse of his bounty, to send rain on your land in season and to bless all the work of your hands. You will lend to many nations but will borrow from none. The LORD will make you the head, not the tail. If you pay attention to the commands of the LORD your God that I give you this day and carefully follow them, you will always be at the top, never at the bottom. (Deuteronomy 28:12–13)

> *My God will meet all your needs according to his glori-*
> *ous riches in Christ Jesus.*   (Philippians 4:19)

God promises to meet my needs, not simply according to the economics of the land but according to His riches—and God is extremely rich. Thus, He has promised abundant supply for my needs.

After I accepted the truth that God had promised me abundance, I also took heed of His warnings for wealth. You see, unlike the blessings of salvation, healing, and deliverance, the blessing of prosperity has dangers attached to it. The dangers of money pulling me away from God are real, and I suppose it was those dangers that made me doubt God's desire for me to have wealth. But I also realized that I could receive plenty and still *"praise the name of the* LORD*"* (Joel 2:26). Material provision would not necessarily make me turn away from Him. On the contrary, it could make me more grateful and God-centered in thankfulness for receiving His blessings. These revelations from the Word of God gave me confidence to pray for success in life. *"Save now, I pray, O* LORD; *O* LORD, *I pray, send now prosperity"* (Psalm 118:25 NKJV). I knew I could always ask the Lord to save me, but now I had confidence also to pray, *"Send now prosperity"*!

Covenants of Confirmation

Let's go back to the story of Abram, who needed additional assurance that God would grant him a land to inherit. God gave him this additional confirmation by making a blood covenant with him. God told Abram to cut some animals in half as an offering. *"On that day the* LORD *made a covenant with Abram and said, 'To your descendants I give this land'"* (Genesis 15:18). This covenant removed all doubt from Abram.

What was a covenant in biblical times? It was a solemn contract ratified with blood. Today, we make contracts to bind people to their word. Two people who make an agreement can shake hands and take each other at their words, or they can sign a contract, legally binding them to the terms of their agreement. The latter is closer to what God did. Even though His word is sufficient, He entered into a blood contract with Abram, assuring him that He would keep His word.

> *Because God wanted to make the unchanging nature of his purpose very clear to the heirs of what was promised, he confirmed it with an oath. God did this so that, by two unchangeable things in which it is impossible for God to lie, we who have fled to take hold of the hope offered to us may be greatly encouraged.* (Hebrews 6:17–18)

This passage identifies two things that are *"unchange-able"*: God does not lie, and He will never break a covenant. It also explains why God made the oath in conjunction with a blood: *"Because God wanted to make the unchanging nature of his purpose very clear to the heirs of what was promised."* Covenants clarify the agreement; God made a covenant to clarify what He had promised.

Since God is sovereign—free to do whatever He wants—He chose to bind Himself in covenant, not just with Abram but also with us. The cross also is a blood covenant promise from God to His people. At the Last Supper, Jesus explained the significance of His imminent death: *"This is my blood of the covenant, which is poured out for many for the forgiveness of sins"* (Matthew 26:28). The Bible is split into two sections: the Old Testament and the New Testament. The word *testament* is a covenantal term. Through God's Word, we can have confidence that He is a covenant-keeping God. He enters into covenant with us so we can have absolute assurance that He will provide for our needs.

A covenant is even greater than a promise or a human contract. In a contract, two parties stipulate the boundaries of an agreement. For example, in a car contract, the buyer promises to pay a certain amount, and the car manufacturer promises to deliver the car, usually with a warranty to cover any repairs needed during the first several years of operation. The contract is not perpetual, nor does it cover other areas of the buyer's life. The manufacturer does not, for example, promise to meet the buyer's needs for finances or good health. It is a limited contract related only to one subject: the car.

In a covenant, however, the agreement covers everything. When two parties make a covenant, they agree that all their assets and liabilities belong to each other. An excellent example of a modern-day covenant is the covenant of marriage. When two people are wed, they enter into a covenant that is all-inclusive. They agree to share everything—for life! This is essentially what God has done. By making a covenant with us, God agreed to take all our liabilities (sins) on Himself through Christ and give us all His assets. This is why Paul wrote, "*We are heirs—heirs of God and co-heirs with Christ*" (Romans 8:17).

In a practical way, God promises to take care of all our needs. It is not necessary for us to know specifically all of what God has promised, since the covenant binds God to take complete care of us. Thus, if you have a particular need that may or may not be specifically mentioned in the Bible, it does not matter. If it is a legitimate need, and if it conforms to the holy life God desires for His children, then you can rest assured that God will meet that need.

Our End of the Covenant

This assurance is not an excuse to ignore God's Word and ask for whatever you want. On the contrary, Jesus established this condition for successful prayers: *"If you remain in me and my words remain in you, ask whatever you wish, and it will be given you"* (John 15:7). Ask whatever you wish—the sky is the limit! But there is a twofold condition: you must remain in Christ, and His words must remain in you. To remain in Him is to live in obedience to Him. To have His Word remain in you is to meditate on Scripture and make it your guide to living. You must be full of the Word. When you are full of the Word, your faith will be strong.

The secret to strong faith in prayer is to make the Word a living reality within you. To do this, you must not treat the Bible as a fairy tale but rather read it as though it is God speaking to you. Many people read the newspaper and believe what they read, yet, when they read the Bible, they doubt it, thinking, *I wish that were really so.* How can you expect to receive answers to your prayers when you struggle to believe the Bible? The Bible is God speaking to you. You need to receive the words of the Bible as the Word of God. Don't doubt their validity.

God and His Word are one and the same. To doubt God's Word is to doubt God. Your contact with God is guaranteed through His Word. It is amazing how few Christians realize this. They have a notion of who God is and what He does, but they base this notion on their own opinions of Him rather than on the Word of God itself. *"Consequently, faith comes from hearing the message, and the message is heard through the word of Christ"* (Romans 10:17). You trust God more when you hear Him speaking to you, and He speaks to you *"through the word of Christ."*

"Sure, Pastor," someone might say, "but men wrote the Bible."

But those men were vessels through whom God spoke. Read this excerpt from one of the men who wrote the Bible:

We also thank God continually because, when you received the word of God, which you heard from us, you accepted it not as the word of men, but as it actually is, the word of God, which is at work in you who believe.

(1 Thessalonians 2:13)

I have never seen a successful person of prayer who did not fully believe that the Bible is the Word of God.

Put God's Word in you, learn what it teaches, and believe all of God's promises. Then, you will have a solid foundation for answered prayer.

Chapter 16

Step Four: Ask and Receive

Give us this day our daily bread.
—Matthew 6:11 KJV, NKJV

It's amazing how shy people are about asking God for what they need. What is it that you need? You must ask for it! And, when you do, you must be specific.

Dr. David Yonggi Cho is pastor emeritus of the world's largest church, in South Korea. Many years ago, when his country was impoverished, he asked God for a bicycle. In a poor country, this was an extravagant request. Several months elapsed, and he did not receive a bicycle. Finally, he asked the Lord why it was taking so long. The Lord answered, *Son, you didn't tell Me what kind of bicycle you wanted. There are many different brands, different colors, and different manufacturers. Be specific. What kind of bicycle do you want?*

We need to be specific in our prayers. Jesus asked a blind man, *"What do you want me to do for you?"* (Mark 10:51). It might seem obvious that the man wanted his sight. But Jesus never presumes to know your desire. He wants you to tell Him.

Someone might ask, "Doesn't the Lord already know what we need?"

Of course He does, but He still tells us to ask Him. That is the legal side to prayer. It is a principle of the kingdom. You must ask.

"You do not have, because you do not ask God" (James 4:2). Let that Scripture sink in. There are things you could be enjoying—health, success, godly children—but you are not, for one reason: *"You do not ask."* Take this Scripture seriously. If you are going to receive everything God has for you, you'd better not be too shy or timid to ask Him.

Dr. Cho began to write out his request for the bike. He got specific. He told the Lord he wanted an American bike with gears to the side so he could regulate the speed. Then, he got even more specific. He threw in a request for a desk and a chair, as well. Joy entered his heart. The next day, he told his congregation, "Folks, by the blessings of God, I have a desk made of mahogany and a chair with an iron frame and rollers on the tips. I even have a bicycle made in the U.S.A. with gears on the side. Praise God!"

The people rolled their eyes. They knew he was poor. But he was doing the same thing as Abram, who believed in a God who *"calls things that are not as though they were"* (Romans 4:17). God changed his name from Abram to Abraham. I envision him telling everyone to call him by his new name, which means "father of many nations." Can you imagine calling yourself a "father of many nations" when you did not have even one child? This is real faith—calling things as they are in the spiritual realm rather than in the natural realm. It was only a matter of time before Abraham's wife, Sarah, became pregnant and their promised son, Isaac, was born, through whom Abraham's countless descendants came.

Dr. Cho, taking his cue from Abraham, told everyone that he had a bicycle and a desk before those items existed in the natural realm. I can only image how Abraham's servants reacted to his name change. In Dr. Cho's case, some young men came up to him after his announcement and said, "Show us the desk and bicycle you have."

Dr. Cho was shocked. He hadn't anticipated anyone asking to see them. He prayed that God would show him how to respond to these young men. God gave him the answer: "When you were conceived in your mother's womb, did you exist?" They all nodded yes. "But you were not seen while in the womb. That is where my desk and bicycle are. They are in my womb. They truly exist, but you can't see them yet."

The men laughed and said, "This is the first time we have heard of a man pregnant with a desk and bicycle." However, they got the point.

This brings us to the importance of receiving as you pray.

Believe It and Receive It

Once you have made a specific request of the Lord, you must believe that you have received what you have asked for, even before you can see it. Remember, Jesus told us to pray, *"Give us this day our daily bread"* (Matthew 6:11 KJV, NKJV). He did not say, "Give us our daily bread." No! He said, *"Give us today our daily bread"* (Matthew 6:11 NIV). You do not wait for *tomorrow* to get the bread you need today. So, when you ask, you must be expectant that the answer is presently being given. In other words, be "pregnant" with the answer.

Jesus said to His disciples, *"Therefore I tell you, whatever you ask for in prayer, believe that you have received it, and it will*

184 Prayers That Get Results

be yours" (Mark 11:24). Notice that this Scripture does not instruct you to believe that you *will* receive. No! It says to believe that you *have* received. This means that you must believe that you already have the answer, even before you possess it, physically or mentally. This is faith.

Believe in Faith

Many times, people pray, thinking they are believing, when, in reality, they are only hoping. Hope and faith are not the same thing. Paul made a distinction between them in 1 Corinthians 13:13: *"And now these three remain: faith, hope and love."* If hope were identical to faith, Paul would not have listed both terms separately in this verse. Yet, many people confuse the words *hope* and *faith*, using them interchangeably. This is incorrect. You have hope for something you look to have in the future, while you have faith for something you claim for yourself now, in the present. You cannot expect to receive from hope what is promised only on account of faith. Faith is what is required for answered prayer.

If you're praying and expecting that God will answer you at some time in the future, then you are not believing in faith but hoping. When you are praying effectively, with belief, you say, "God has answered my prayer the very moment I pray." Are you believing or hoping?

Believe for Today, Not Tomorrow

I'm reminded of a story that Happy Caldwell once told. Before he was saved, he and his buddies used to love getting drunk. One day, they were driving down an Arkansas highway when they passed a run-down tavern. A sign in the window read, "Free Beer Tomorrow!"

They got excited. They could hardly wait to guzzle down all that free beer.

The next day, they sped back to that old tavern, and the sign was still in the window. They jumped out of their car, burst through the tavern door, and shouted, "Hey! Give us some free beer!"

"What are you talking about?" the bartender asked.

The guys pointed to the sign. "You are advertising free beer. That's what we've come for."

The bartender smiled and pointed to the sign. "Free beer—*tomorrow*!" They had been tricked.

The devil is like that bartender. He will make you think that you will get your answer tomorrow. But when tomorrow arrives, he says, "Wait until *tomorrow*." As long as you are waiting for tomorrow, tomorrow never arrives. God says, "Believe that you have the answer today—NOW!" This is what Jesus meant when He said, *"Whatever you ask for in prayer, believe that you have received it, and it will be yours"* (Mark 11:24).

If you are not pregnant, you are not going to give birth. Many women want to give birth, but they do not wish to conceive or endure nine months of pregnancy. Likewise, many people want to receive answers to their prayers without first getting "pregnant" by receiving the answers in their spirits. You have to believe you have the answer inside of you. If you don't, you will never "give birth" to the answer.

Rejoice and Be Thankful While You're Waiting

Someone may ask, "How long will I have to believe I have the answer before I give birth to it and finally see it?" To be honest, you may have to wait a long time. Instead of being concerned with the length of your spiritual pregnancy, simply give thanks to God. I believe that joy-filled thankfulness is a good way to trigger the "contractions" of this birthing process.

Some people pray a lot but are quite negative and pessimistic. They seem to wait a long time before they see any answers to their prayers. You must learn to be thankful and joyful right now, even though you still feel the painful symptoms, even if the money has not arrived, even if your spouse is still ignoring you. You cannot go on what you see. *"We live by faith, not by sight"* (2 Corinthians 5:7). Expectant parents do not wait to rejoice until after the baby is born; they begin celebrating even before the baby is conceived. Later, after conception has been confirmed, the husband might even touch his wife's abdomen and say, "Oh, I feel the baby moving. It's kicking." They are happy, even though they cannot see the baby, because they know the baby is real at conception.

The only reason you are not happy in your life is that you do not see the healing, prosperity, and other blessings of God as real. You think of them only as wishes and hopes, not as realities. They aren't real to you because you have not received the Word inside your spirit. The Word is the seed. When that seed is fertilized inside your heart, conception takes place. But, as long as you try to conceive the answer without the Word, you will remain discouraged.

Mary immediately rejoiced when the angel told her that she would give birth to the Son of God. Before her body had undergone any changes as a result of her pregnancy, she exclaimed,

> *My spirit rejoices in God my Savior, for he has been mindful of the humble state of his servant. From now on*

*all generations will call me blessed, for the Mighty One
has done great things for me.*   (Luke 1:47–49)

Only days after she had heard the angel's promise, Mary
already was declaring with joy that she was with child.

Why can't you do the same?

Act like You are Blessed

"*Do not be anxious about anything, but in everything, by
prayer and petition, with thanksgiving, present your requests
to God*" (Philippians 4:6). Again, you must present your requests "*with thanksgiving.*" I am thankful for the blessings I
have received. But you might say, "I have not yet received the
blessings." Really? I thought you were pregnant. You have received the blessings, and that is why you must thank God for
what He has given you. You must act like you are blessed.

Even in the natural, we learn to be thankful before people actually complete the promises they have made to us. For
example, if someone comes to you and says, "I want to buy
you some new furniture," what is your response? Naturally,
you thank the person, even though he has not yet purchased
any new furniture for you. You thank him right away—you
don't wait to thank him until the furniture has been delivered to your house. If you observe this practice with your fellow man, why not observe it in your prayers to God, who is
faithful to meet all your needs? The moment you ask God for
something He has already promised to you, thank Him right
away, knowing that He will do what He said He would.

Chapter 17

Step Five: Forgive/Repent

And forgive us our debts, as we forgive our debtors.
—Matthew 6:12 KJV, NKJV

Little Johnny was playing in the sandbox with a schoolmate. They were laughing and having fun when the schoolmate threw some dirt at Johnny. Johnny angrily stormed out of the sandbox and went to play on the swing set. Less than five minutes later, Johnny went back to the sandbox and resumed playing with his schoolmate as if nothing had happened. This is how children act. They may offend one another, but they soon forget the offense and reestablish their friendship.

Jesus said, *"I tell you the truth, unless you change and become like little children, you will never enter the kingdom of heaven"* (Matthew 18:3). Recall your own childhood. You probably got into yelling matches with your brothers and sisters or schoolmates. You may have become angry with your parents, from time to time. But you were likely always quick to forgive, even if you did not realize it at the time. You found yourself once again playing with your siblings and friends, as if nothing negative had ever happened.

As we grow older, however, we lose the childlike ability to let go of past wrongs committed against us. We are "older and wiser," and we hold on to the wrongs, as if that were the "smart," "adult" thing to do. In reality, we are acting foolishly and unwisely.

Paul said, "*In regard to evil be infants*" (1 Corinthians 14:20). Infants are innocent. They are unaware of good and evil. So, when other people treat you evilly, look at their actions through the eyes of innocence. Instead of holding those people accountable for their actions and harboring a grudge against them, choose instead to treat them as if they were innocent.

Avoiding the Hindrance of Unforgiveness

It is not a coincidence that Jesus included forgiveness in His instructions on how to pray. Unforgiveness is the number one hindrance to answered prayer. In another teaching, Jesus said, "*And when you stand praying, if you hold anything against anyone, forgive him, so that your Father in heaven may forgive you your sins*" (Mark 11:25). When you are praying, if you have not forgiven others, your prayers will not work.

In the contemporary church, there is an overemphasis on seeking God's forgiveness, yet lamentably little mention about the importance of forgiving others. The church, in all of its denominations, has focused primarily on vertical forgiveness—asking God to pass His forgiveness down to us—and has neglected the message of horizontal forgiveness—extending forgiveness to, and receiving forgiveness from, our brothers and sisters in Christ.

For instance, a Catholic believer enters the confessional and is assigned some penance to make up for his misdeeds. Little thought is given to confessing the hurts and bitterness he feels toward those who have wronged him. Instead, confession is focused strictly on our standing with God, in regard to our personal sins.

The same trend is happening in the Protestant church. Even in the full-gospel church where I grew up, I did not hear much from my pastor about forgiving others. In fact, he even admitted to hating that part of the gospel. Yet, he was a great soulwinner. He was constantly giving altar calls for salvation to which thousands of people responded. But he was cut from the same cloth as the Catholic and Protestant churches. To be fair, my pastor mentioned the need to avoid strife, but he gave no specific instructions to forgive other people. All the while, below the surface, members of my church were seething with resentment toward those who had offended them or hurt their feelings in some way. While they definitely needed to receive forgiveness for their sins, their need to forgive others was sorely neglected.

We are the products of the teachings we receive. If we do not hear about the requirement to forgive others, how can we strive to obey it? That is why this chapter is so essential. I am aware of the lack of teaching on the importance of forgiving others. Except for a few special Bible teachers, most church leaders neglect this vital commandment in the Bible—and at the peril of the souls of their congregants. No one should be surprised by ineffective prayers if he or she will not forgive others.

Examine Your Heart

If my prayers are not receiving answers and reaping blessings, the first thing I do is examine my heart to see whether I am harboring resentment, bitterness, or unforgiveness against anyone. I do not want anything to hinder my prayers, especially unforgiveness.

During this "heart checkup," the first area I examine is my relationship with my wife. Have I been harsh toward her? Am I holding an unrecognized grudge against her? The apostle Peter warned husbands that if they did not treat their wives properly, their prayers would not be heard. *"Husbands, likewise, dwell with them with understanding, giving honor to the wife, as to the weaker vessel, and as being heirs together of the grace of life, that your prayers may not be hindered"* (1 Peter 3:7 NKJV).

Your prayers can be *"hindered"* if you do not treat your spouse with sensitivity. Husbands, have you been harsh with your wife? Do you see her from God's perspective? Do you make her cry and hurt her feelings? If so, you have seen the results: God knows how you treat her, and He has not answered your prayers.

Remember That God Forgave You

"Be kind and compassionate to one another, forgiving each other, just as in Christ God forgave you" (Ephesians 4:32). Forgiving others is tied directly to God's forgiving us. When we came to Christ, God forgave us for all our sins, as we experienced His mercy and grace. Jesus endured the punishment we deserved so that God could lavish us with unmerited blessings. We do not deserve any of this. It is all God's grace. Likewise, the success of our prayers is based on grace.

The Bible says, *"Let us then approach the throne of grace with confidence, so that we may receive mercy and find grace to help us in our time of need"* (Hebrews 4:16). The throne of God is also the *"throne of grace."* It is here that we *"receive mercy and find grace."* It is not called a "throne of merit." We do not ask for justice or for the punishment we deserve. If you desire grace and mercy from God, yet you do not extend grace and mercy to others, you disqualify yourself from the privilege of having access to the throne of grace.

The world does not understand the gospel's requirement to forgive everyone, because they have not personally experienced God's forgiveness. But we, as followers of Christ, have experienced forgiveness, and so forgiving others is a requirement.

A few years ago, Focus on the Family founder Dr. James Dobson did a radio interview with David Works and Ronald Murray, whose children had been killed in a tragedy at New Life Church in Colorado Springs, Colorado, in 2007. David Works' daughters, Stephanie and Rachel, were shot and killed by Donald Murray's son, Matthew, at the church. After shooting the girls and wounding three others, including David Works, Matthew was wounded by a church security officer and then took his own life.

The interview was poignant. These two men were sitting directly across from each other when Dobson asked David Works how he felt toward Ronald Murray.

Works replied, "He lost a child, too. It was not his fault."

Dr. Dobson asked Works if he could ever forgive Matthew Murray for killing his two daughters. Works said, "Forgiveness was never an option for me. It was mandatory. Long ago, before the murders took place, I settled that I would forgive anyone who wronged me. Matthew is no exception."

If there was ever someone with a reason to be bitter, it was David Works. But he forgave. His reasons were clear. He himself had been forgiven for all his sins, and, in turn, he made it a policy to forgive everyone of any sins they had committed against him. No exceptions; no excuses. He forgave. Period.

I like how David Works expressed the act of forgiving others as "mandatory." In college, there are both mandatory and elective courses. Electives are not required. They are usually the classes you enjoy the most. However, it's the mandatory courses you take that ultimately qualify you to earn your specific degree. Similarly, in the Christian life, there are optional electives—choosing a particular spouse, for example—and there are mandatory courses. One such mandatory "course" is forgiveness. It isn't a matter of choice. If you want to graduate from the school of prayer, you first must pass the test of forgiveness.

Let Go of Petty Grievances

Many of us hold on to petty grievances. It's often hard to believe how such seemingly insignificant issues could cause so many serious problems. Consider the following list of the main reasons people become bitter toward others:

1. *Receiving unsolicited advice.* This is the number one reason people get offended. Someone gives you unsolicited advice, and you become upset. *How dare he butt into my life?* you think to yourself. Or, *Who asked her opinion?*

2. *Feeling insulted.* Someone makes a comment that causes you to feel belittled in some way. Maybe it was the tone of voice that caused this feeling, or you may feel offended by a perceived slight. *I can't believe they seated me so far from the bride and groom,* a wedding guest might think with indignation. *Well, I never!*

3. *Feeling excluded.* You were not invited to the party, and so you feel bitter, believing that your resentment will "punish" the person who left you out.

4. *Feeling let down.* You expected something from someone, but he did not deliver. You take it personally.

5. *Feeling betrayed.* You entrusted a secret to someone, and that person went and told someone else.

6. *A broken promise.* Someone promised to take you to a concert but never called. You feel rejected or ignored.

Believe it or not, these are the top reasons people take offense and harbor bitterness against others. Yet none of the slights on this list, whether perceived or real, could cause serious physical harm to anyone. The damage they do is emotional, and it happens as a result of the way people react to them.

We would understand resentment from someone who suffered true harm—someone who was robbed at gunpoint, or someone who, like David Works, suffered the tragic loss of a loved one. Yet, ironically, most cases of resentment do not stem from legitimately painful experiences.

Jesus illustrated the folly of unforgiveness in a story about a servant who was forgiven a debt of millions of dollars by the king. Immediately afterward, the servant grabbed the throat a friend who owed him a few dollars and demanded he pay what he owed. (See Matthew 18:23–35.) God is the King who has forgiven us of the huge debt we could never repay; meanwhile, we, when we practice unforgiveness, are the servant who grabs the throats of those people who owe us a few dollars—in other words, who commit petty offenses against us—as if they owe us millions of dollars in reparations. How distorted is this way of thinking!

Follow the Bible's Commands

"Jesus said, 'Father, forgive them, for they do not know what they are doing'" (Luke 23:34). The most common excuse people give for withholding forgiveness is this: "He hasn't said he's sorry!" Whenever I hear this excuse, I ask, "So, did you point out this person's errors, and he refused to repent?" Most people respond, "Well, no, I haven't told him how he hurt me. He should just know."

As Jesus said, some people *"do not know what they are doing."*

If someone has hurt you, yet you haven't even attempted to tell that person how you feel, then you have failed to follow Jesus' command to *"go and show him his fault, just between the two of you. If he listens to you, you have won your brother over"* (Matthew 18:15).

"But, Pastor," you may protest, "I don't want to make matters worse by confronting him."

Fair enough. But until you speak privately to that person about what he did to hurt you, you have lost your right to speak of how he has hurt you. Unfortunately, most people skip this first step of reconciliation and go directly to their spouses, friends, and family members to tell them what the offender did to them. This is an act of unforgiveness.

You may insist, "But what he did was wrong. I can't keep quiet about it." Then, again, talk to the person privately. Most people will repent when confronted with their mistakes. If you are not willing to take this first step, you have no right to take any further steps. You cannot bypass this step!

Even if you have taken all of the steps the Bible lays out in regard to reconciliation (see Matthew 18:15–17), and the individual who hurt you refuses to repent, you still have to forgive him for the sake of your own soul. Remember, God will not forgive you if you don't forgive others! And why should you allow an unrepentant person to rob you of peace and power with God? Don't let unforgiveness keep your prayers from being answered.

Avoiding the Hindrance of Cherished Sin

"*If I had cherished sin in my heart, the Lord would not have listened*" (Psalm 66:18). We now turn to the issue of our own sin, which we deal with through "vertical forgiveness." God will not listen to us if we "cherish" sin in our hearts. Notice, this verse does not say that God will not listen to our prayers if we sin. If that were the case, none of our prayers would ever be answered. No, it says, "*If I had cherished sin....*" The word "*cherish*" means "to care for" or "to delight in." It is to protect something; to have a high regard for it. At most traditional weddings, the vows exchanged by the bride and groom include the statement "I promise to love, honor, and *cherish* you." To cherish someone is to hold that person in the highest favor and esteem.

Truly Repent

If someone "cherishes" sin in his heart, he will do anything to protect his right to keep on sinning. He may even flaunt his sins. This type of person, who disobeys God on purpose, should not expect his prayers to be answered.

On the other hand, sinners who hate their own sin— those who repent of sinful behavior—can rest assured that God hears their prayers. It is entirely possible to sin and, at the same time, hate the very sin being committed. Paul described this experience in Romans 7:15: "*For what I want to do I do not do, but what I hate I do.*"

Some people sin because of addictions and compulsions seemingly beyond their control. They may act impulsively and commit a sin, only to regret it later. These people, who are not proud of the sins they commit, can trust that God will open His ears to their prayers for deliverance.

King David is a good example of someone who cherished sin. He lusted after his married neighbor Bathsheba, committed adultery with her, and then tried to cover it up, but that was hard to do, since she had conceived a child as a result of their interlude. So, he arranged for her husband's murder and then married Bathsheba. She gave birth to a son, who soon became sick. David prayed intensely for the child to recover. Yet, even though David was a man after God's own heart (see Acts 13:22), God did not intervene, and the child died.

The problem was clear: King David had cherished lust for Bathsheba in his heart. He did not want anyone to pray with him regarding his weakness. He did not seek help or deliverance until his son was already conceived and born. God did not intervene to save the child from sickness because David's actions had made his enemies show contempt for Israel and her God. (See 2 Samuel 12:13–14.) As a result, David ultimately suffered the consequences of his sin.

Ask God to Search Your Heart

Here is an appropriate psalm to pray when you are unsure of whether you are cherishing or hating your sin, which was written by David:

> Search me, O God, and know my heart; test me and know my anxious thoughts. See if there is any offensive way in me, and lead me in the way everlasting.
> (Psalm 139:23–24)

Don't rely only on your own abilities to discover any hidden sin in your life, for that will just cause you to become guilt-ridden and frustrated. Instead, allow the gracious Lord to search your heart. Ask Him to point out any offense that you may have committed, in word, thought, or deed. You can be sure that if He finds something, He will work to purify you from it. Do not be afraid of His purifying methods, because He has a way of cleansing us without hurting us.

David's final request was this: *"Lead me in the way everlasting."* This is the greatest request to ask. All of our prayers should point in this direction. When you desire eternal life more than anything else, it is doubtful that you will cherish sin for very long. Eventually, you will repent of it, and, when you do, your prayers will be answered.

Chapter 18

Step Six: Engage in Spiritual Warfare

And lead us not into temptation, but deliver us from evil.
—Matthew 6:13 KJV

The word translated as "*evil*" in the above verse is a personal noun. It literally means "evil one," which is how the *New International Version* translates the term. God is not the tempter but the deliverer. Many times, though, when it seems that our prayers are taking a long time to get answered, we may be tempted to think that God is withholding the answer. In many cases, though, it isn't God who's keeping the answer from coming; it is the devil.

The devil will keep the symptoms increasing while you pray for health.

The devil will keep the money from coming while you pray for prosperity.

The devil will keep the strife in your marriage while you pray for harmony.

The devil will keep your mind oppressed while you pray for deliverance.

The devil will keep your heart depressed while you pray for joy.

The devil will keep your congregation from growing while you pray for increase.

If you are going to see your prayers answered, you must defeat the devil. When you have done everything you know to do, and still your prayers are receiving no answers, you must fight the evil one!

Defeating the Strong Man

"When a strong man, fully armed, guards his own house, his possessions are safe" (Luke 11:21). There are three things you must do to protect your possessions in Christ:

1. You must be stronger than Satan.

2. You must be fully armed against him.

3. You must guard your own house.

In a fight, the stronger opponent usually wins. This means you must be stronger than Satan if you are going to defeat him. How can you be stronger than Satan?

> *...I write to you, young men, because you are strong, and the word of God lives in you, and you have overcome the evil one.*   (1 John 2:14)

"Young men" is a reference to new believers. Even a new believer can become stronger than Satan. The apostle John told them—and he tells you, too—*"You are strong."* And, because you are strong, you can *"overcome the evil one."* How does a new believer become strong? John told us in the middle of this verse: *"the word of God lives in you."* That's the key. The Word of God is stronger than Satan.

I used to watch the cartoon *Popeye the Sailor Man* as a child. Popeye was no stronger than anyone else. He was an ordinary sailor—until he ate his spinach. Whenever he gobbled down a can of spinach, he grew stronger than anyone else. That is a good way to illustrate the strength of the new believer. We may be no stronger than any other person. And, on our own, we are certainly not stronger than Satan, who started out as an angel. Even though he became a fallen angel, he retained some of his power and abilities. As such, he is much stronger than we are in the natural realm. However, when we feed on the Word of God, we become stronger than Satan. One punch from our fist can send him across oceans. But we are stronger than Satan only when we've eaten our "spinach"—the Word of God.

Eat Your "Spinach"—the Word of God

Without a steady diet of the Word of God, you are susceptible to the attacks of the evil one, and he is sure to defeat you. *"If you falter in times of trouble, how small is your strength!"* (Proverbs 24:10). One sign of small spiritual strength is faltering in times of trouble. To falter is to make missteps or to give up entirely. The word also carries with it the idea of failing under pressure.

Trouble will come to you, in every realm of life: your family, your home, your work, your church, and elsewhere. And it is what you do in the midst of trouble that indicates your spiritual strength. Life is 10 percent what happens to you and 90 percent how you react to it. If you speak negatively or react out of fear, it is a sign that your spiritual strength is small—you haven't been eating your "spinach." If, however, praises are springing forth from your heart, and your reactions to adversity are based on faith, then your strength is great.

I just finished reading the story of Brother Yun, a Chinese believer who has suffered enormous persecution for his faith—thrown into prison, beaten to the point of death, spit on, urinated and defecated on, and abused in every possible way. Yet, through all of this, he has joyfully maintained his faith in the goodness of God. As I read his story, I couldn't help but think of the vast number of American Christians who abandon their joy and faith in God's goodness in the face of the most insignificant of problems. These people will call it quits just because of an ingrown toenail. They'll throw in the towel on their marriage because their spouse works too much. They'll leave the church they've been attending because they don't like a particular person. They end up on the verge of suicide if they lose their job or their boyfriend or girlfriend breaks up with them.

When someone is quick to give up in the face of trouble, it shows how little the Word of God means to him. He has not been eating his spinach. The Word is not living in him. It is not enough to merely hear the Word preached in your church on Sundays; you must have the Word *living in you*. In order for this to happen, you need to give God first place in your life and make it your top priority to study His Word. Nothing should mean more to you than Scripture. No one's opinion should override what the Word teaches. No circumstance should deter you from following the Word. No temptation should entice you to disobey it. Nothing should move you, because the Word of God lives in you.

Fully Arm Yourself

The second step in building spiritual strength and overpowering Satan is to "fully arm" yourself, according to the apostle Paul's instructions:

Finally, be strong in the Lord and in his mighty power.
Put on the full armor of God so that you can take your
stand against the devil's schemes. For our struggle is not
against flesh and blood, but against the rulers, against
the authorities, against the powers of this dark world
and against the spiritual forces of evil in the heavenly
realms.   (Ephesians 6:10–12)

Our real battle in prayer is not against an unbelieving
spouse, a disobedient child, a political party, or a neighboring
church that seems to be attracting bigger crowds on Sunday
mornings. Our battle is with the devil and *"the spiritual forces
of evil."* The way we take our stand against these forces is by
putting on *"the full armor of God."*

God's armor is greater than any weapon Satan has at his
disposal. Satan's arsenal of weapons includes sin, condemna-
tion, sickness, lack, discouragement, fear, depression, anxiety,
and so on. But God's armor enables us to withstand any of
Satan's schemes.

Thinking about the armor of God always reminds me of
the first time I saw the movie *Raiders of the Lost Ark* in a
movie theater. In one scene, Indiana Jones meets a large man
in a black robe who is intent on killing him. The man gives
an evil grin and begins swinging a large saber back and forth
with lethal ease. Indiana Jones has no sword. Every person in
the theater with me was on the edge of his seat, wondering
how our hero would escape this predicament. As the scene
continues, Jones simply lets out a deep sigh, pulls out a gun,
and shoots the menacing thug. At this, the audience broke
out in riotous laughter. We were shocked by such a simple yet
effective solution.

In the same way, God's armor outranks every weapon in the devil's arsenal. The issue for the believer is to make sure he or she puts on the full armor of God. It will do you no good to leave your armor hanging in the closet. It's meant to be worn and used!

The Belt of Truth

Stand firm then, with the belt of truth buckled around your waist.... (Ephesians 6:14)

In biblical times, a soldier's belt held sheaths for weapons, such as knives and swords. To wield a sword, a soldier first had to be wearing his belt, where he kept that particular weapon. Just as the starting point of physical warfare was a soldier's belt, the starting place of spiritual warfare is the *"belt of truth."* The only way to wield any spiritual weapon successfully is to first "buckle up" with the belt of truth, or be grounded in the truth. This groundedness is crucial if we are to recognize the devil's number one scheme, which is deception.

The devil begins every attack by lying. Jesus called him *"the father of lies"* (John 8:44). Yet his deceptive schemes are no match for the power of the Holy Spirit in our lives. Thus, there is no need to stand against the devil in your own power. The only real influence Satan can exert over you is deception through his schemes. This is why truth is more important than power. Many believers keep praying for more *power*, when what they really need is more *wisdom*, because wisdom is based on truth. When you know the truth, you will not fall for Satan's lies.

Some of Satan's favorite falsehoods are that God is not to be trusted and that His Word is not true. It's no coincidence that the Scriptures come under attack more often than the person of Christ. Many people say, for example, "I believe in Christ, but I have doubts about the Bible." What they forget is that the Bible is the means by which we come to know Christ. You cannot separate the two. In Jesus, *"the Word became flesh and made his dwelling among us"* (John 1:14). You cannot succeed in spiritual warfare if you doubt the Bible. The Bible is God's Word, and it is truth.

The Breastplate of Righteousness

> *...with the breastplate of righteousness in place....*
> (Ephesians 6:14)

Righteousness is right standing with God. With righteousness you have rights. Had our nation's founding fathers used Old English terminology, the Bill of Rights would have been called the "Bill of Righteousness." However, you lose your sense of confidence to claim your rights when you feel guilty. Guilt is a great enemy of effective prayer. Scripture calls Satan *"the accuser of the brothers"* (Revelation 12:10). He schemes to make us think that God has not forgiven us. This is why it is essential to put on the breastplate of righteousness. By doing this, you remind yourself that God has forgiven your sins and considers you righteous in His sight. When you put on the breastplate of righteousness, you quit dwelling on your past mistakes!

Some people make the mistake of equating their righteousness, which has been imparted by God, with "righteous" acts they have performed. While righteous behavior is commendable, even our best actions are tainted by sin; as the prophet Isaiah put it, *"all our righteous acts are like filthy rags"*

(Isaiah 64:6). There is nothing we can do, in our own power, to make ourselves righteous before a holy God. Righteousness is a gift, and it comes from Him alone.

> *Now when a man works, his wages are not credited to him as a gift, but as an obligation. However, to the man who does not work but trusts God who justifies the wicked, his faith is credited as righteousness.*
> (Romans 4:4–5)

There are two ways to receive money. Either you *earn* it, or you *receive* it as a gift. Righteousness works in the same way. Paul wrote of two kinds of righteousness: one comes from man's works, and the other is God's gift. Yet man can never perform enough righteous works to be right in God's sight. The only reason man can stand righteous in God's sight is because of Jesus' redeeming work on the cross. "*God made him who had no sin to be sin for us, so that in him we might become the righteousness of God*" (2 Corinthians 5:21). True righteousness is a gift from God, and it's our job to receive it. However, if you insist on basing your righteousness on right behavior, then you will struggle with a guilty conscience because of the sins you will inevitably commit. And a guilty conscience keeps you from praying with confidence. Therefore, you must put on the breastplate of righteousness—the type that comes from God, in spite of—and because of—the sins you have committed.

The Gospel of Peace

> *And with your feet fitted with the readiness that comes from the gospel of peace.*
> (Ephesians 6:15)

Shoes may not seem like much of a weapon, but try marching into battle without them. Paul was encouraging us to be ready to share our faith whenever God gives us an opportunity to do so. Sharing the gospel with others may not seem like a tactic of spiritual warfare, but it is. When you share the gospel, you bring people out of darkness and into the light.

"I pray that you may be active in sharing your faith, so that you will have a full understanding of every good thing we have in Christ" (Philemon 6). The more active we are in sharing our faith with others, the more fully we understand every good thing we have in Christ. I can testify to the validity of this truth. Some of the greatest revelations I have ever received have come to me while I was preaching the gospel. Not to sound pompous, but I have grown significantly through my own preaching. And this is true for anyone who spends a great deal of time sharing the gospel of peace. The more you preach, the more you learn.

One other thing should be mentioned here. Paul instructed us to have our *"feet fitted."* We do not all wear the same shoe size. I think we need to learn to share the gospel in our own "shoe size"—according to our own unique style. Instead of trying to copy other people, be yourself when you share the Word. Don't try to be Billy Graham or Kenneth Copeland. Just be the person God created you to be, and you will reach the audience for whom you were fashioned.

The Shield of Faith

Take up the shield of faith, with which you can extinguish all the flaming arrows of the evil one.

(Ephesians 6:16)

The devil is on the offensive. He is going to send you trials and tests. And the only way to overcome those tests and trials is through faith. Faith is the positive expectation that God is going to perform something you desire. It is *"being sure of what we hope for and certain of what we do not see"* (Hebrews 11:1). You need this positive expectation, especially when the enemy is shooting his flaming arrows in your direction. Those arrows may take the form of sickness, poverty, hardship, or other difficulties. But, through faith, you can deflect those arrows and extinguish them. The fire will be snuffed out, and you will triumph. The key is to resist the inclination to give in to fear and expect the worst to happen.

A negative mind-set gives Satan an advantage over you. It causes widespread damage, such as is caused by a flaming arrow. On its own, a regular arrow is ineffective if it misses its target. Light it on fire, though, and it's likely to ignite whatever it hits: a thatch roof, for example. Soon, the fire spreads to neighboring houses, just like a nasty attitude is prone to be passed from one person to the next. If you persist in your negative expectations, Satan's arrows will waste no time burning up other areas of your life, as well as the lives of others. I have watched people lose a lot more than just income after being let go from their jobs, all due to a negative mind-set: their health, their marriages, and more. Everything collapses when you expect the worst. So, take up the shield of faith and deflect the arrows of the enemy.

Love as a Breastplate

Let us…[put] on faith and love as a breastplate….
(1 Thessalonians 5:8)

Faith and love work together. You shouldn't exercise an attitude of faith for your own life alone; it's crucial to have a faith-filled attitude toward the situations of your brothers and sisters in Christ, as well. This is where love comes in. You must seek the best in every person. Just as you believe the best will happen in your life, you must believe the same concerning the lives of others. This is love.

I imagine that few people would consider love as a spiritual weapon. Yet love is the greatest weapon of all. When you love others and treat them the way you would want to be treated, Satan can't attack you. If you love your enemies, as Jesus commanded you to do (see Matthew 5:44; Luke 6:27, 35), you will ward off the flaming arrows of the devil.

Paul summed it up well in his letter to the Romans:

If your enemy is hungry, feed him; if he is thirsty, give him something to drink. In doing this, you will heap burning coals on his head. Do not be overcome by evil, but overcome evil with good. (Romans 12:20–21)

The Helmet of Salvation

Take the helmet of salvation.... (Ephesians 6:17)

Let us...[put] on...the hope of salvation as a helmet. (1 Thessalonians 5:8)

Of all bodily injuries, the most serious ones occur to the head. This is why a helmet is the most important piece of protective gear you can put on in potentially dangerous situations. Likewise, the worst spiritual injuries occur in the head—specifically, the mind—especially when a saved person thinks he has lost his salvation.

Annabelle was losing her mind because she thought she had forfeited her salvation. A voice in her head kept telling her to curse the Holy Spirit. As she plunged deeper into depression, she uttered a prayer: "I just wish the Holy Spirit did not exist."

After this, she became fearful and paranoid that she was going to lose her life and go to hell. Then, she attended a retreat, where she wrote a note on a piece of paper: "I hope God sends someone to tell me that God loves me." On the third day of the retreat, a man Annabelle had never met before said to her, "Did you know that God loves you?" Just then, the bondage broke from her life. She was free.

The fear of losing their salvation plunges many people into the depths of despair. Every week, I receive letters from people telling me that they have committed the "unpardonable sin." Many of them have psychiatric problems. It's easy to see how "head injuries" occur when people doubt their salvation. In these cases, the head injuries are in the form of mental illness. Yet, these mental illnesses are preventable, just as physical head injuries are often preventable. The way to protect yourself from losing your mind in this way is to always affirm your salvation. Know that once you have been saved, you will remain saved. Affirm this truth as often as you can, even if it means wearing a physical helmet as a reminder.

The Sword of the Spirit

> Take...the sword of the Spirit, which is the word of God. (Ephesians 6:17)

The sword of the Spirit is your only offensive weapon. Ultimately, you must be on the offensive. You can't always be fighting off Satan and trying to hold your ground. You have to move forward and take *his* ground. And you do this by speaking the Word of God. The sword of the Spirit came out of Jesus' mouth, as we read in Revelation 1:16: "*In his right hand he held seven stars, and out of his mouth came a sharp double-edged sword.*" This is how you fight on the offensive in spiritual warfare. You *speak* the Word of God.

Speaking the Word of God is the most valuable thing you can do in the midst of a spiritual battle. Remember that Jesus spoke the Word of God when He was tempted by Satan in the desert. (See, for example, Luke 4:1–12.) The difference between having the Word in your *heart* and having the Word in your *mouth* is commitment. You make a firm commitment with your mouth. If you are married, you made a commitment through the speaking of vows to pledge your fidelity to your spouse. When you speak the Word of God, you commit to believing it and seeing it through to the end. Many, however, do not commit to standing on the Word of God. Their negative confession betrays the Word in their hearts.

When answers to prayer seem to take a long time, many believers alter their request or drop it altogether. If it seems that a prayer for healing has failed to materialize, for example, they say, "Well, I guess I'll just have to learn to live with this illness until I die." Instead of making a negative confession, they should confess the Word of God and say something like, "By Jesus' stripes, I am healed. This sickness will not end in death. I shall live and declare the glory of the Lord." (See 1 Peter 2:24; Psalm 118:17.) Your positive, faith-filled confession that is based on the Word of God keeps you on the offensive. In time, Satan's attacks will not cause any further damage, and the harm that has already been done will be removed.

Guard Your House

The last point Jesus made in Luke 11 concerning our war with the devil is that when the child of God *"guards his own house, his possessions are safe"* (Luke 11:21).

The Bible gives us many pictures of God's people, portraying them as a legislative assembly, a family, a temple, a bride, a city, and so forth. One of the most striking pictures is that of an army engaged in battle. Yet this analogy uncovers a great error among many sincere believers who presume that God causes or allows every single event that happens in their lives, and so they do nothing to change their circumstances. If these people perceive that their prayers are not being answered, they assume that God must not want to answer them. They fail to realize that the devil is behind the delay. Satan will do everything in his power to block the will of God from being fulfilled in their lives.

It is for this reason that you must "guard your own house" from the attacks of the enemy. God's first instruction to Adam in the garden of Eden was to *"work it and take care of it"* (Genesis 2:15). The Hebrew word for "take care of" is *shamar*, meaning "to keep," "to guard," or "to observe." This word carries the implication that an enemy exists who will try to rob Adam of his place in the garden, and that Adam must not surrender to him. Of course, we know that the devil succeeded in tempting Adam and Eve to sin, which resulted in their expulsion from the garden. Adam and Eve forfeited the inheritance God had intended for them to enjoy.

The devil tries to do the same thing with you. He tries to get you to forfeit your inheritance. He does this by attempting to convince you not to take spiritual warfare seriously. He wants you to become passive and accept whatever happens as the will of God instead of putting up a fight by standing on God's promises, as laid out in His Word.

Do not be lulled into this deception. Guard your house and protect your inheritance.

Suppose you hear a knock on your door and, when you open it, a man bursts inside wheeling a dolly and starts loading it with your furniture. Would you simply stand there and let him take away all of your furnishings? Of course not! You would say, "Hey, what do you think you're doing? This is my house and my furniture. You get out of here!"

Yet, the devil comes to us and tries to wheel away all of the possessions and promises God has given us. Too often, we sit back and let him, as we say to ourselves, *Oh, well. The Lord giveth and the Lord taketh away.* (See Job 1:21.) No! Jesus told us to pray, *"Deliver us from evil"* (Matthew 6:13 KJV). In saying this, we acknowledge the existence of a devil who opposes us. And, if we acknowledge him, shouldn't we try to fight him?

Don't just let the devil walk over you. Put up a fight! Stand your ground! Just because you have not yet received an answer to your prayer does not mean it will never come. If you are standing on a promise from God, stay strong and fight; you will see the answer in God's perfect timing.

"I will give you every place where you set your foot, as I promised Moses" (Joshua 1:3). God has made many promises to you, but, like Joshua, you must *"set your foot"* on them. Lay claim to them. Joshua had to fight off enemies who tried to keep him out of the Promised Land. He defeated the people of Jericho, Ai, and many others.

Too often, Christians tire of fighting and become passive. They want everything to come easily. You will never develop an effective prayer life until you build up a fighting spirit that perseveres through every spiritual battle.

Conclusion:

How to Pray the Lord's Prayer

In the preceding pages, you have learned what took me decades to discover about prayer. Of course, I stood on the shoulders of giants in the faith, from whom I learned nuggets of truth about how to pray successfully. This book represents the accumulated knowledge and experience I gleaned from some of the greatest teachers of the Word. Thanks to the wisdom of those who have gone before us, you have the opportunity to learn more about prayer in this one source than previous generations could ever have hoped to learn. Don't let it go to waste. Let me offer some final thoughts about prayer.

Prayer is meant to be two-way communication. It is not just about you talking to God; it is also about letting Him talk to you! In a two-way conversation, it is best to let the smarter one do most of the talking. God is infinitely smarter than you, so you would do well to let Him dominate the conversation. This means that you should spend more time reading His Word than talking to Him. Jesus said, *"If you remain in me and my words remain in you, ask whatever you wish, and it will be given you"* (John 15:7). A key to successful prayer is meditating continually on the Word of God. I spend more time studying the Word and hearing from God through it than I do talking to God. Getting into the Word is part of prayer, so, you must include this practice as part of your prayer time.

Take the advice of Solomon: "*Do not be quick with your mouth, do not be hasty in your heart to utter anything before God. God is in heaven and you are on earth, so let your words be few*" (Ecclesiastes 5:2). Jesus warned against "*vain repetitions*" (Matthew 6:7 KJV). He said, "*Do not keep on babbling like pagans, for they think they will be heard because of their many words*" (Matthew 6:7). Long, verbose prayers are not necessary to get God's attention. To be heard by God, it takes only an honest, heartfelt appeal that is based on His promises.

This is not an excuse to neglect extended times of prayer, however. Jesus was known to spend all night in prayer. (See Luke 6:12.) Someone might wonder how it is possible to spend even one hour in prayer, let alone an entire night. It is not hard to do when you have a prayer program—a template, of sorts, to guide your words. And that's exactly what Jesus gave us in the Lord's Prayer. We explored aspects of the Lord's Prayer as the foundation of "Steps to Answered Prayer" in Part III. Now, we will look at various parts of Jesus' prayer as a guide to our times of personal prayer.

> *In this manner, therefore, pray: Our Father in heaven, hallowed be Your name. Your kingdom come. Your will be done on earth as it is in heaven. Give us this day our daily bread. And forgive us our debts, as we forgive our debtors. And do not lead us into temptation, but deliver us from the evil one. For Yours is the kingdom and the power and the glory forever. Amen.*
>
> (Matthew 6:9–13 NKJV)

In the Lord's Prayer, Jesus gave us a series of simple, memorable phrases to encapsulate the subjects we should cover in prayer. This prayer, as He taught it to His disciples, consists of fewer than seventy words and takes no more than a minute to utter in its entirety. But Jesus did not intend for us to pray it hastily or by rote. Rather, the Lord's Prayer was intended to work more like a zip file on a computer, if you can get past the anachronistic comparison. A zip file compresses computer data so that it takes up less space on your computer. Zip files, however, cannot be read as they are. You must have a program that "unzips" them and grants you access to their contents. Similarly, the Lord's Prayer is compressed. You must "unzip" the prayer in order to unlock its rich treasure trove of truths.

The Five "Destinations" of the Lord's Prayer

On the popular TV show *The Amazing Race*, contestants race around the world to far-flung destinations using various means of transportation. In the Lord's Prayer, there are five destinations, each of them marked by a short phrase. At each of these destinations, you can take an in-depth tour of the great truths behind the brief words used to identify it. You don't live in just those specific words any more than you live at the airport of a city. You get out of the terminal and explore the great sights to be seen. With the Lord's Prayer, you disembark from the words and explore their meanings. You can spend hours at each destination. This is how to develop a meaningful prayer life that will endure through the years.

First Destination: "Our Father"

The Lord's Prayer begins, "*Our Father in heaven, hallowed be Your name*" (Matthew 6:9 NKJV). Catholics simply call the Lord's Prayer the "Our Father," or "Paternoster" in Latin. I actually think this is good. It reminds us of whom we are praying to. Many see God as the Creator, but Jesus made Him more personal. He is our Father. How intimate! You can spend a lot of your prayer time just thanking God for the blessing of being born again and being able to call Him "Father." A good father cares for his children. A father undertakes the responsibility of providing for all of his children's needs. In this short phrase, *"Our Father,"* Jesus told us a lot about God. Our God feels responsible for us, His children, and will meet our needs.

The next phrase reminds us of God's holy—or *"hallowed"*—name. Names reveal a lot about a person's character. If you meet someone called "Dr. so-and-so," you have a good idea of what he does for a living. Jesus knows there is no point to praying until we know what God will do for us. In Scripture, God's many names reveal His work in our lives.

God revealed Himself to Moses, and when Moses asked His name, God replied, *"I Am Who I Am"* (Exodus 3:14). This biblical terms "Yahweh," "Jehovah," and "Lord" are derived from the Hebrew word for *"I Am."* In this sense, this instance marked the first time God revealed Himself as Lord of our lives. Later, through time, God added to our understanding of His Lordship.

He called Himself Jehovah-Rophe, meaning *"I am the Lord who heals you"* (Exodus 15:26). Therefore, it is proper to go to God for health and healing because He is your Physician.

He called Himself Jehovah-Tsidkenu, meaning *"The Lord Our Righteousness"* (Jeremiah 23:6). God is the One who pardons you and makes you right in His sight. He is your Savior, to whom you run for mercy.

He called Himself Jehovah-Shalom, meaning "The Lord is Peace" (Judges 6:24). He can calm your emotions. He can bring an end to the wars and strife in your life. He is the God of peace.

He called Himself Jehovah-Shammah, meaning "The Lord is there" (Ezekiel 48:35). When you pray, God is not far off in the sky somewhere but right there beside you. If He is with you, there is no need to be afraid or to feel powerless over your circumstances.

He called Himself Jehovah-M'kaddesh, meaning "I am the Lord, who makes you holy" (Exodus 31:13). When you struggle with sin, God will help you to overcome the temptation. He can make you holy.

He called Himself Jehovah-Nissi, meaning "The Lord is my Banner" (Exodus 17:15). Banners are lifted up because of victory. God is the One who gives you the victory over all your battles.

He called Himself Jehovah-Rohi, meaning "The Lord is my shepherd" (Psalm 23:1). A shepherd is a caretaker. He keeps the wolves away from the sheep; he feeds them and guides them. Whatever a shepherd does for his sheep, God will do for you.

He called Himself Jehovah-Jireh, meaning "God himself will provide" (Genesis 22:8). When it seems like you do not have enough, God comes through for you. He meets your every need, whether it's physical, material, spiritual, mental, or emotional.

As you can see, you can have a wonderful time in prayer by just recounting all of God's wonderful covenantal names.

Second Destination: "Your Kingdom Come"

The second destination in the Lord's Prayer is as follows: "*Your kingdom come. Your will be done on earth as it is in heaven*" (Matthew 6:10 NKJV). This is not a request but a demand. In other words, it is a declaration that God's will is going to be done. This means that the will of God must be made known. What does it mean for the kingdom of God to come on earth? "*For the kingdom of God is not a matter of eating and drinking, but of righteousness, peace and joy in the Holy Spirit*" (Romans 14:17). The Holy Spirit ushers the kingdom into our lives by bringing righteousness, peace, and joy, which are among the fruits of the Spirit. (See Galatians 5:22–23.) He also brings forth the gifts of the Holy Spirit. (See 1 Corinthians 12.) "*For the kingdom of God is not a matter of talk but of power*" (1 Corinthians 4:20).

When I pray, I like to remind God of all the gifts of the Spirit that I desire to see manifested in my life. This takes some time to do, but it is an exhilarating exercise that builds my faith when I pray to the Lord and expect all His gifts to be developed in my life.

Of course, through it all, I submit myself to do the will of God. I recognize that I am not on earth to do what I want but what God wants. I begin to think of what God wants me to do—witness to someone, write an article, lay hands on the sick, or something else—and then I devote myself to doing it. When I take these matters to the Lord in prayer, I have confidence that He will perform His will through me.

Third Destination: "Give Us Our Daily Bread"

The third destination of the Lord's Prayer is found in these words: "*Give us this day our daily bread*" (Matthew 6:11 NKJV).

It is not selfish to pray for your personal needs. God wants you to ask Him, and you should do so unashamedly. *"Bread,"* of course, represents whatever material needs you may have. Do you need money for a car payment? A lower interest rate for your mortgage? Ask Him!

"Bread" also represents health and deliverance. Jesus called health *"the children's bread"* (Matthew 15:26). So, you can seek the Lord in prayer and ask Him to heal you. You can ask Him to deliver other people from demon possession. All of these things are covered in your *"daily bread."*

The most important "bread" is the Word of God. As you feed yourself on His Word, ask Him to give you fresh insights into His truth, and He will gladly open the *"eyes of your understanding"* (Ephesians 1:18 NKJV).

Fourth Destination: "Forgive Us"

The fourth destination of the Lord's Prayer is this: *"And forgive us our debts, as we forgive our debtors"* (Matthew 6:12 NKJV). God's mercies are new every morning (see Lamentations 3:22–23 NKJV), and we need a fresh supply of His forgiveness on a daily basis, sinful people as we are. So, we should pray this prayer daily. Do not think you have ever gone a day without sinning—or even a minute. Something that you did, said, thought, or spoke missed the mark. You may not be aware of any specific sins, but ask God to forgive you, anyway.

During this part of the prayer, I like to remind myself of my earthly failures, which brings me to a place of humility. I am not suggesting that you carry around a guilty conscience and always beat yourself up about your failures, but it is a healthy practice to make note of your shortcomings. It gives you a perspective of humility and a greater empathy for others, which makes it easier to pray for them. It also makes it easier to forgive other people.

It's easy to focus on others' sins. We're quick to dredge up the past and almost enjoy dwelling on the ways in which others have hurt us. Yet we struggle to remember our own sins, whether past or present.

After I have confessed whatever sins I remember committing each day, big or small, I am more than ready to forgive anyone for any sins that he committed against me. I release every one of his debts because I remember how many of my own debts God has forgiven and forgotten. I am grateful for God's mercy and happy to extend it to others.

Fifth Destination: "Lead Us Not into Temptation"

Our fifth destination is this: *"And do not lead us into temptation, but deliver us from the evil one"* (Matthew 6:13 NKJV). I realize that deliverance is better than forgiveness. While I will always rely on God's mercy and ask Him to forgive me, I also pray that I will not sin or otherwise offend Him. I ask for deliverance.

As I spend time in this destination, I am keenly aware of the spiritual battle in which every believer is involved. So, I put on the full armor of God and take a stand against the devil. I know my armor is greater than Satan's. He is no match for God, nor me, for that matter, since I trust in God.

Back to the Beginning:
"For Yours Is the Kingdom"

The last part of the Lord's Prayer, *"For Yours is the kingdom and the power and the glory forever. Amen"* (Matthew 6:13

NKJV), is not a separate destination but a returning home. It reminds us of what our prayers are meant to accomplish—the glorification of God through our lives. After I have prayed my way through the Lord's Prayer, touring the great truths of these words, I leave my prayer closet ready to live victoriously for the Lord.

You have the same ability. You don't have to wonder why this prayer wasn't answered or that prayer received an answer different from what you were hoping for. The reason is that you have shifted your hope from this world to the next, and the perspective of eternity causes you to step back and trust God in all things. Prayer is meant to prepare you for that better world, where, for all of eternity, we will be giving God the praise for all things. In that day, answered prayers will take on a new meaning. You will not be looking for health, wealth, or restoration. You will have arrived at a place of utter contentment in God. For now, however, you have this road map to prayer. It is the Lord's Prayer. Take the map and follow it—unzip it and explore it—and you will start seeing your prayers answered.

About the Author

Tom Brown is best known for his deliverance ministry. Millions have seen him on ABC's *20/20*, as well as on MSNBC and the History Channel. He is a noted conference speaker, prolific author, and committed pastor. His award-winning Internet site, www.tbm.org, reaches more than a million people each year. His previous books include *You Can Predict Your Future; Devil, Demons, and Spiritual Warfare;* and *Breaking Curses, Experiencing Healing*. Tom is most committed to his wife Sonia and three children: Justin, Faith, and Caleb. Tom and Sonia are empty nesters living in El Paso, Texas.

DON'T MISS
RACHEL FRIEDMAN'S
NEXT ADVENTURE

Rachel is determined to make this the
best Hanukkah ever . . . no matter what!

9/3/2024